Curriculum at Your Core

Curriculum at Your Core

Meaningful Teaching in the Age of Standards

LAUREN POROSOFF

A Division of
ROWMAN & LITTLEFIELD
Lanham • Boulder • New York • London

Published by Rowman & Littlefield
A wholly owned subsidiary of The Rowman & Littlefield Publishing Group, Inc.
4501 Forbes Boulevard, Suite 200, Lanham, Maryland 20706
www.rowman.com

16 Carlisle Street, London W1D 3BT, United Kingdom

British Library Cataloguing in Publication Information Available

Library of Congress Cataloging-in-Publication Data Available
ISBN 978-1-4758-1310-4 (cloth : alk. paper)— ISBN 978-1-4758-1311-1 (pbk. : alk. paper)—
ISBN 978-1-4758-1312-8 (electronic)

♾™ The paper used in this publication meets the minimum requirements of
American National Standard for Information Sciences—Permanence of Paper for
Printed Library Materials, ANSI/NISO Z39.48-1992.

Printed in the United States of America

Contents

Preface

The Values That Guided This Book

I'm a teacher, and I wrote this book for teachers. The anthology *Poetry Speak Who I Am* (Paschen and Raccah 2010), which we use in my seventh grade English class, begins: "This is not a poetry anthology for adults, for children, for classroom study, or for required memorization and recitation. It's made just for you" (xiii). This is not a curriculum design book for administrators, for school officials, for mandatory in-service days, or for required adoption and implementation. It's for you.

I want this book to be applicable to you whatever grade and subject you teach, so I've done my best to provide examples and case studies from lots of grade levels and subject areas, including the traditional "academic" subjects as well as music, the arts, and physical education. Since one of my own greatest values is genuine inclusion, I've tried to write about ideas that apply to all subjects and grade levels and, if a particular discussion applies more to some subjects and grade levels than others, I've tried to say so.

In the interest of conciseness, I don't always include multiple examples to illustrate a point, but I know it can be hard for, say, high school teachers to see themselves in a story about a second grade teacher having his students make a dinosaur mural. Also, since many of the stories in this book are based on what I have experienced in my own classroom or witnessed firsthand at the schools where I've worked, middle school and humanities are somewhat overrepresented. I hope you'll be able to see how these examples pertain to your work.

Since it's important to me that you'll be able to use what's in this book, rather than giving you just the framework and examples and then leaving you to sort out how to make them work for you, I've included exercises, protocols, and templates you can use alone and with colleagues to write and assess your own curriculum.

I also wanted to account for how schools are complicated social institutions with potential conflict at every level. Maybe you've watched school leaders' efforts to force change or create "buy in" met with reluctant compliance or vocal resistance. This book assumes and even celebrates that not everyone in a school will think the same things are important and that the diversity among teachers can be a source of creativity and strength. The protocols are made especially to encourage inclusive participation and critical reflection when groups of teachers work together so they can design curriculum they all stand behind.

I also trust that you're willing to tinker with your curriculum and develop something better. When I bought my smartphone, it wasn't because my old flip phone was *broken*; I wanted something better. You're not saying about your curriculum, "If it ain't broke, don't fix it." I imagine you as someone who wants to teach with integrity and serve your students well by designing more meaningful learning experiences. I wrote this book because I hope it will help you do that.

Acknowledgments
The Evolution of This Book

This book never would have existed without the compassionate mentoring that Melanie Greenup gave me. She sent me to workshops, handed me books, and spent many hours talking to me so I'd develop the skills to write better curriculum and to support colleagues in writing theirs. Melanie sees clearly and almost clairvoyantly what people are supposed to do with their lives. I feel tremendously grateful for her wisdom and kindness, and I dedicate this book to her and to mentors like her.

Laurie Hornik is a brilliant teacher and a supportive colleague. She shares her ideas generously, and she helps me return to my values and improve my practice. She also gave frequent and thoughtful (and sometimes funny) comments on even the bad early drafts of this book.

My husband, Dr. Jonathan Weinstein—besides being a loving partner and watching the kids while I wrote—introduced me to functional contextualism, applied behavioral analysis, and the way values are used in acceptance and commitment therapy. These became foundational ideas for this book.

Workshops at the Bard Institute of Writing and Thinking, especially those Carley Moore and Abby Laber led, taught me ways teachers can discover and deepen their ideas. The "values rendering" and writing-to-think exercises in this book apply Bard Institute practices to curriculum design.

Eric Baylin and his colleagues at the Packer Collegiate Facilitative Leadership Institute taught me how critical friends protocols encourage trust and inclusive participation among teachers who don't necessarily share values.

Barbara Swanson, the associate director for professional development at the New York State Association of Independent Schools, helped me put forth workshops for which I created and used the protocols and examples in this book. I also thank the workshops' participants for their feedback and their tireless work to improve their practice.

My colleagues at the Charles E. Smith Jewish Day School, the Maret School, and the Ethical Culture Fieldston School inspire me with their excellent teaching. I thank them all, and especially those whose names and stories are used in this book: Ellie Bibas, Jason Ford, Debbie Kriger, Laurie Hornik, Vincent Lebrun, Tony Marro, Jeff Nurenberg, and Jon Riches. I also thank the colleagues who, over the years, have worked closely with me on curriculum: Dina Weinberg, Janet Gocay, Kalin Taylor, Renee Price, Lauren Keller, and Dori Kamlet Klar.

Tom Koerner and Carlie Wall at Rowman & Littlefield gave careful attention and suggestions that made this book so much better. I also appreciate the time and thought contributed by the reviewers of this work: John Baglio, Cathy Burns-McDonald, Harry Chaucer, Laura Danforth, Jay Heath, Laurie Hornik, Kevin Jacobson, Steve Noga, Marie Pagliaro, Harriet Porton, Renee Price, Kate Reynolds, Elizabeth Scott, Dina Weinberg, Jonathan Weinstein, and Jessica Wolinsky.

Thanks to my parents, Leslie and Harold Porosoff, and my children, Allison Porosoff and Jason Weinstein, for their love and support.

Finally, thanks to every student who's been in my class. I hope I've taught them something they value.

Introduction

Why values?

Creating a curriculum means identifying the set of understandings, knowledge, and skills that is most important for students to learn. What gets called "most important" depends on values. Teachers and administrators, missions and charters, school boards and standards, professional and parent associations, and students themselves all make pronouncements about what's "most important" to learn. These are values statements.

Some teachers have predefined images of what good teaching looks like and aim to make their work look as much like these images as possible. In a philosophy called formism, there is some predefined image (or form), and something is "good" if it looks like that image (Fox 2006). An English teacher shows students how to identify the prepositions in a sentence because that's part of what it means to be an English teacher.

This book is rooted in a different philosophy, functional contextualism. In a functional contextualist approach to education, teachers aren't holding their teaching, classrooms, or curriculum up to a predefined form; they're trying to make important learning happen, and what learning is deemed "important" depends on values (Biglan and Hayes 1996; Hayes, Hayes and Reese 1988; Fox 2006). How "good" a curriculum is depends on how well it gets students to know and do what's deemed important.

According to functional contextualism, an English teacher shows students how to identify the prepositions in a sentence because it serves important values: it helps students write clearer prose, or it allows them to score well on tests that influence their futures, or it gives them all access to the same knowledge. In turn, the preposition lesson is a "good" lesson if it works—if it serves its valued purpose.

Imagine you have one of those cheap plastic ballpoint pens, and you manage to use it until it completely runs out of ink. At that point, you decide this pen is garbage (or at least recycling) because it "doesn't work." If your purpose is to write, the pen isn't valuable at all. But you might imagine situations where a pen with no ink is *more* valuable than a pen with ink. A sculptor might think the pen with no ink is better because he can scrape clay out from under his fingernails without getting them inky.

One thing—whether it's a pen or a lesson on prepositions—might have many imaginable purposes, but you'll say it "works" if it serves the purpose you value.

CURRICULUM THAT SERVES MULTIPLE SETS OF VALUES

People get their values from a slew of influences: their families, friends, teachers, neighborhoods, cultures, religious backgrounds, and personal experiences. Much has been written elsewhere about how school evolved into what it looks like today (Kliebard 2004; Ravitch 2011; Urban and Wagoner 2014) and arguing that schooling needs to be restructured to match twenty-first-century imperatives (Jacobs 2010; Darling-Hammond 2010; Slattery 2013). Curriculum is a construct designed to serve multiple, shifting sets of values.

The writers of the Common Core State Standards (NGA Center for Best Practices and CCSSO 2010) value ensuring "American students [are] fully prepared for the future [so that American] communities will be best positioned to compete successfully in the global economy." The influential philosopher Paulo Freire (2000) argues that education should be a process of collaborative knowledge construction: the "restless, impatient, continuing, hopeful inquiry human beings pursue in the world, with the world, and with each other" (72).

So, which is the "real" purpose of curriculum: to prepare young people to be competitive in the global marketplace or to strive for knowledge through cooperative inquiry? Whether you agree with one, both, or neither of these perspectives—or the perspective of any person or institution—will depend on your values. Values themselves cannot be right or wrong, but actions can be consistent or inconsistent with a particular set of values.

Thus, according to functional contextualism, there are no "essential" questions, "best" practices, or "core" standards; there are only the values people bring to their work and how well the work serves those values in the context of their surroundings. This book is about finding more effective ways to serve your values and any other values that guide your teaching: those embedded in standards, missions, and charters, as well as those your colleagues, students, parent and professional associations, and communities hold.

A PLACE AT THE TABLE: YOUR VALUES AND THE STANDARDS

If your focus is on standards and test scores, you might be skeptical about the place of *your* values in planning curriculum. The very idea of talking about your values might sound lofty, cute, or pointless—perhaps even offensively so, if your job and your school's funding are on the line. You might feel you need to "stay on book" (to borrow a theater term); that is, you stick to the standards and let them tell you what to cover in your class.

But for one thing, no matter how standards-compliant, research-backed, or "teacher-proof" your curriculum is, you're the actual person in the actual classroom with the actual kids, and your values will come through. You teach who you are, and you matter.

For another, it's possible to write curriculum that serves multiple sets of values. Thus, references in this book to "your" values include both the individual "your" (the values belonging to *you*, the teacher) and the collective "your" (the values you are serving as part of a department, team, school, or district).

As for the standards, Christine Sleeter (2005) distinguishes between what she calls standards-driven and standards-conscious curriculum planning. In standards-driven planning, the teacher treats the standards as if they *are* the curriculum and tries to get through them all before test time, while in standards-conscious planning, "the standards are a tool, but not the starting point, and do not define the central organizing ideas and ideology of one's curriculum" (60).

The Common Core is a values-based document. This book is designed to work with any set of values, including and not limited to those embedded in the Common Core. This book is not anti-Core, but if it sounds like it is, that's because some schools implement standards-driven curriculum to the exclusion of teachers' ability to use their expertise and creativity in crafting meaningful curriculum that serves other sets values, too.

You might think of the standards in the same way you'd think of a dietary guide to how much of each nutrient to take in each day. Dietary guides tell you what you need to get out of your meals, but they don't tell you what to put on the menu. In planning a week of dinners, you might make sure you're getting the protein and vitamins you need, but you probably don't *start* by looking at dietary guides; you start by pulling out a favorite recipe or seeing what's fresh at the market.

Curriculum planning can work in much the same way. Instead of starting with a set of standards, you can start with your values: what do you think is important about the topic you're asking your students to consider? As you plan your unit, you can consult the standards to make sure you're meeting them and adjust your curriculum as necessary.

USING THIS BOOK

Getting clear on values gives you a starting place to design curriculum that ensures meaningful learning, so this book begins with materials adapted from contextual psychology to help you clarify your values as a teacher (chapter 1) as well as those of your students, colleagues, and institution (chapter 2).

The next few chapters are about how to use values as a starting point to design cohesive, outcome-oriented units of study: how to articulate what about a topic is most important for students to learn (chapter 3), organize the unit into meaningfully sequenced lessons (chapter 4), create an assessment tool that will make valued learning visible (chapter 5), and make sure the lessons and assessments work together to serve the unit's purpose (chapter 6).

The later chapters account for how curriculum design becomes more complicated at each level of the system, moving from units to courses (chapter 7) to subject-based and grade-level programs (chapter 8), across disciplines (chapter 9), and over time (chapter 10). These chapters show how values can guide you in designing units in the context of the larger curriculum.

1

Clarifying the Values That Guide Your Teaching

What do you most want for your students, and how do you let that guide your teaching?

Henry, a second grade teacher, spends a week during the summer learning how to teach course content through the arts. In one workshop, each teacher researches a fish from the Great Barrier Reef in order to make a collaborative mural. The teachers learn how to gesso a huge piece of particleboard and then paint it to resemble water. Then, they make line drawings of their fish, trace the drawings onto transparencies so they can project them onto the water background, retrace them there, and paint them. They show interrelationships by painting predators lurking by their prey and symbiotic organisms helping each other.

The mural is stunning, and in the process of making it, Henry finds himself learning a lot about the fish of the Great Barrier Reef. Even years later when the movie *Finding Nemo* comes out, Henry immediately recognizes the butterfly fish he'd painted. More importantly, Henry is inspired. His second grade class begins the year with a unit on dinosaurs. Instead of having the children make dinosaur A-to-Z booklets as a culminating project, how wonderful would it be to have them paint a three-panel mural of the Triassic, Jurassic, and Cretaceous periods?

Driving home from the workshop, Henry gets more and more excited thinking about the mural. It would give his students an authentic reason to read about different dinosaurs and other Mesozoic wildlife, and the separate panels would tangibly show how not all dinosaurs lived at the same time. The kids would think critically about how dinosaurs related to each other and to their surroundings. He could show pictures of impression fossils to give the students a sense of a dinosaur's skin texture, and since there's no way to know what colors dinosaur were, the students could look at pictures of dinosaurs' closest living relatives, birds, to get ideas.

Planning this project fills Henry with vitality. The mural would engage the students. (Who wouldn't have fun painting an enormous turquoise-and-orange dinosaur?) It would allow everyone to participate and contribute. It would elicit curiosity and critical thinking, and it would create an authentic context for thoughtful reading, research, planning, and cooperation. It would help the students remember the content better than if they made dinosaur booklets as his classes had in the past. As much as he loves the summer, Henry is looking forward to September because he knows his curriculum will fit so many of his values.

WHAT VALUES ARE (AND AREN'T)

When people and institutions name their values, they often use abstract nouns like "integrity" "creativity," and "excellence." You can't hold or point to creativity, though you can point to a person who's approaching a math problem creatively or making creative choices in how she draws a landscape. In order to describe *living* your values, you need to add a verb to the abstract noun: "*using* creativity," "*acting* with compassion," "*fostering* an atmosphere of excellence." A "good" curriculum will be one that allows you and your students to do what you think is important, making these abstractions manifest.

Psychologists who write about values often distinguish between values and goals (Hayes and Smith 2005, 159; Harris 2009, 192; Wilson and DuFrene 2009, 67–68): unlike goals, which can be checked off a to-do list, values are ongoing.

For example, if a math teacher wants to make a project that will give her students a deeper understanding of percentages, that's a goal. Once she makes the project, she's done. She could set a new goal of improving the project so it better promotes the students' understanding, but that's another goal. If she wants to make sure her students can use math in their daily lives, that's a value—an ongoing process she can engage in every day from now until she retires.

Values also aren't mere preferences. Teaching by your values means you're creating opportunities for students to engage in learning processes and reach outcomes you believe to be important. The fact that you enjoy assigning a cute activity or discussing a particular topic with your class doesn't necessarily mean your students are doing important work. Living by your values often brings deep satisfaction and vitality, but the day-to-day effort of committing to values doesn't necessarily feel pleasant and sometimes feels like a burden (Yadavaia and Hayes 2009).

Take a history teacher who values clear communication and continual growth. In long comments on students' essays, he points out specific examples of where they have and have not been clear and suggests strategies for improving clarity in future writing. All that commenting can feel tedious, but the teacher is pursuing his values. When his students write their next essays, they consult his comments, apply his suggestions, and grow in their ability to communicate clearly.

Conversely, if this same teacher enjoys the feeling of being the center of attention, he might do a lot of storytelling in class. Though he feels delighted upon hearing his students laugh and gasp at his stories, he's not necessarily pursuing teaching values in those moments. If he's spending so much time telling stories that his students are missing opportunities to develop their own communication skills, then this teacher's pursuit of his own good feelings actually gets in the way of pursuing his values.

Finally, values describe how people genuinely *want* to behave. Some math teachers make sure their students learn how to use math in their daily lives not because they value it but because they were taught that way and don't know any differently, or because an administrator told them to, or because the Common Core says everyone should. These aren't bad reasons for taking action, but they aren't the same as acting in accordance with values. You live by your values not because you feel compelled by guilt, fear, written or unwritten rules, or the desire to please someone else, but because they give meaning to your life—in this case, your teaching life.

CLARIFYING YOUR VALUES AS A TEACHER

When you think about your teaching, what's important? What matters most to you? What kind of teaching do you want to do? Even those who are particularly self-aware might have trouble rattling off their values if asked. Textbox 1.1 is a brief writing exercise designed to help you think about what matters most to you in your teaching.

TEXTBOX 1.1

WRITING TO CLARIFY VALUES

Choose one or more of the prompts and try to write for at least five minutes. If you get bored or have nothing to say, switch prompts. The point is not to write beautifully or say the "right" thing but to find your values.

1. Imagine your retirement party. What do you hope your colleagues or administrators will say in their speeches? You can write the actual speeches or just write about what they would say.

2. Imagine the thank-you note you most wish a student or parent would write to you at the end of the year. What would it say? You can write the thank-you note itself or just write about what it would say.

3. Who is a colleague you look up to? What does this colleague do that inspires you? What are this colleague's strengths that you admire?

4. What do some of your colleagues do in their classes that you disapprove of or resist? What would you do differently if you taught their classes?

5. Make a list of "Magic Moments in ___" (filling in the blank with the name of the course you teach).

Writing about your work from a student's or colleague's perspective might free you to say things you wouldn't want to say about yourself because it would feel like bragging. Imagining the end of the year, or even the end of your career, lets you clear away the moment-by-moment challenges of your school life and pay attention to what you truly want to stand for as a teacher. Based on this vision of your ideal future, can you create some statements about your values?

Another way to think about your values is in terms of your colleagues. If you have colleagues who inspire you or fill you with admiration, their actions might tell you something about the teacher you hope to be. That doesn't mean you have to do exactly what your colleagues do or live up to some standard you think they set.

Vincent is a brilliant French teacher who is also a talented musician and performer. He uses music to get his students comfortable with French pronunciation, vocabulary, and grammar. Some of his colleagues are in awe of his teaching, some shrug and say, "I could never do that," but some try to figure out what about Vincent's teaching they value: maybe finding imaginative ways to facilitate learning, appealing to a wider range of students, creating a stimulating atmosphere, and helping students master the material. These are things all teachers can do in their classes, with no musical or French-speaking skills required.

On the flip side, you might have colleagues who teach in ways you doubt or even oppose. The point of writing about them isn't to say mean things or dwell on who's "right"—it's to notice your feelings of disapproval or resistance, because these are signs your own values are being compromised. Using your feelings of admiration or disapproval as guideposts, can you make some statements about your own values?

You might prefer to focus on concrete, specific images of the past and present (as opposed to visions of an ideal future) and on your own classroom and practices (as opposed to your colleagues'). Identifying moments that have felt magical helps you discover the values that were being served in those moments. What are some of these values?

When you're finished with the values clarification exercise, you could choose to share some part of what you wrote with a trusted colleague or friend. It can be very powerful to say your values out loud to another person. If you do, notice any times you want to justify, qualify, or disclaim something you say. That's an indication that you're judging your values as "right" or "wrong." As Russ Harris (2009) puts it, "Values are beyond right or wrong, good or bad. They are simply expressions of what matters to us" (193).

MAKING VALUES STATEMENTS

Some teachers find it easy to use the values clarification writing prompts but still have trouble getting from their writing to expressions of what matters to them. Textbox 1.2 has a list of things teachers sometimes say they value. It's not a list of the "best" values; it's here just to provide examples. Feel free to borrow as much or as little as you want from the list in creating statements of what matters most deeply to you.

TEXTBOX 1.2

EXAMPLES OF VALUES

Since teaching by your values is an ongoing set of behaviors, not a thing you can have or a goal you can achieve, try putting verbs such as "acting with," "teaching with," "showing," "fostering," or "ensuring" in front of the abstract nouns you choose as your values.

Accountability	Empathy	Modesty
Accuracy	Enthusiasm	Novelty
Achievement	Equity	Openness
Activity	Excellence	Patience
Adventure	Faith	Peace
Appreciation	Flexibility	Perspective
Authenticity	Freedom	Practicality
Autonomy	Generosity	Presence
Awareness	Grit	Prudence
Beauty	Hard work	Reliability
Boldness	Harmony	Resilience
Choice	Honesty	Resourcefulness
Clarity	Hope	Respect
Closeness	Inclusivity	Responsibility
Compassion	Independence	Restraint
Competition	Individuality	Self-control
Confidence	Innovation	Self-examination
Connectedness	Integrity	Simplicity
Cooperation	Involvement	Sincerity
Courage	Joy	Skill
Creativity	Judgment	Status
Curiosity	Justice	Success
Dedication	Kindness	Sustainability
Deference	Knowledge	Tact
Determination	Leadership	Thoroughness
Directness	Love	Trust
Diversity	Loyalty	Variety
Efficiency	Mastery	Wisdom

RENDERING VALUES FROM ACADEMIC DOCUMENTS

In cooking, "rendering" means cooking a piece of meat until the fat melts out in order to use the fat for something else, like rendering the fat from bacon and using it to sauté chicken. Text rendering, which was developed at the Bard Institute of Writing and Thinking, is a way to get something meaningful or useful out of a text. Schools are full of texts: syllabi, assignments, course descriptions, mission statements, charters, and standards. Any of these documents can communicate the author's values. Textbox 1.3 presents a protocol for rendering values from academic documents.

AVOIDING YOUR VALUES

After his mural workshop, Henry jots down some ideas for his dinosaur unit and gets on with the rest of his summer, excited for the school year to start. Then, the school year actually does start.

TEXTBOX 1.3

VALUES RENDERING PROTOCOL

This protocol is adapted from text rendering experiences led by Carley Moore at the Bard Institute for Writing and Thinking (2010–2013).

1. Choose an academic document written by you, or by your department, team, school, district, or state. Read it with a group.
2. Each person underlines phrases that seem particularly striking or important. These don't have to relate to the overall topic or purpose of the document; they only need to seem meaningful or stand out in some way.
3. Each person numbers three underlined parts: 1 for most striking or important, 2 for second-most striking or important, 3 for third-most.
4. Going around in a circle, everyone reads their 1s.
5. Everyone reads their 2s.
6. Everyone reads their 3s.
7. The group has a discussion about the document, using these questions:

   - What did you notice when you heard the text in this way?
   - What does the person or group who wrote this text seem to value?

Henry begins telling himself stories. *I don't have the time to do such a huge project. I'm not a real muralist. It sounds like a lot of work to get all that paint. Where do you even buy gesso? And I can't even fit one piece of particleboard in my car—much less three. All of this will cost money. And the other second grade teachers will never want to do this. It's not like I can just do it without them—they'll get mad! And what about the teacher who shares my room with me? There's no way she'll want three boards taking up space. Forget it. We can make A-to-Z booklets like we always have. They work just fine.*

Henry's story isn't unique. The psychologist Kelly Wilson (2009) points out that no one lives in accordance with their values all the time: "Some days, some moments, we will be well-oriented within that pattern [of living by our values]. Other days, other moments, we'll find ourselves at odds with our value. In that moment, the moment in which we notice that we're out of alignment with our value, can we pause, notice our dislocation, and gently return? It's difficult to imagine a value of any magnitude that will not involve a lifetime of gentle returns" (70).

In that spirit, try the Values Self-Assessment (table 1.1) where you state your values, rate how important they are to you at this moment, and rate how consistently you've been living by each of these values in your current work as an educator. The values clarification exercises in chapter 1 will help you come up with statements that describe your values.

BARRIERS TO TEACHING BY YOUR VALUES

When you did the self-assessment, were there any values you rated higher for "importance" than "consistency"? The point of noticing when you're not as successful as you'd like to be in teaching by some of your values is an opportunity—if you're

Table 1.1. Values Self-Assessment

Write a phrase or statement that summarizes your value as an educator.	Rate on a scale of 1–10 how important this value is to you personally at this point in time.	Rate on a scale of 1–10 how consistently you're currently living by this value in your work as an educator.

Adapted for educators from The Valued Living Questionnaire (Wilson et al 2010).

willing—to begin that "gentle return." Dr. Russ Harris (2009, 32), who also does work around values, identifies four kinds of barriers to valued living.

Getting Stuck in Self-Limiting Beliefs

People think self-limiting thoughts all the time. They believe they can't do something that matters to them because of some deficit within themselves ("I'm not smart enough," "I'm just not a creative type") or some aspect of their personal or professional identities that they feel is in conflict with the action they want to take ("Math teachers don't teach writing," "I don't do that touchy-feely stuff").

It doesn't actually matter whether these self-limiting thoughts are true; what matters is whether you use these thoughts to stop you from teaching by your values. It's true that Henry isn't talented artistically, all the know-how he has about muraling comes from a day-long workshop, and he isn't good at getting his second grade colleagues to embrace his ideas. But the question isn't whether your beliefs about yourself are true. The question is whether you can imagine a world where these beliefs *are* true and you act in accordance with your values anyway.

A belief about yourself also doesn't have to be negative to be limiting. Imagine if Henry were great at drawing and that he'd devised the booklet-making project that the second grade has done for years. Maybe he'd have thoughts like, *Our project is already brilliant. Anyway, I'm a better artist than the kids. They'll be intimidated when they see my example.* These beliefs are positive in a certain sense, but they could still get in Henry's way—unless he chose to believe them and do the mural anyway. Can you imagine a world where teachers think highly of their teaching and materials, and still try something new that could be even better?

Avoiding Uncomfortable Feelings

Feelings like frustration, embarrassment, and exhaustion aren't fun, but they're sometimes a necessary part of living your values. Setting up a mural project would take time and effort: to go to the hardware store, haul the materials to school, tape garbage bags to the floor to protect it from paint, find resources about Mesozoic flora and fauna, put students into groups, and deal with both the inevitable "I wanted the apatosaurus!" tantrum and his colleagues' iciness if he does the mural without their blessing. Using the booklet project would let him avoid these annoyances and fears, but avoiding these feelings would mean avoiding his values.

Disregarding What Matters Most

This is good old-fashioned rationalization. Henry tries to convince himself that the students will be fine making A-to-Z booklets; surely they learned something last year and weren't *harmed* by the project. Though the booklets aren't a collaborative project, he reasons, some students prefer to work alone, and though making a picture book of alphabetized dinosaurs doesn't show which dinosaurs lived at which times or how they interacted with their surroundings, it helps kids develop language skills. Right?

Telling himself these kinds of stories might let Henry get away with ignoring how much he cares about innovation, authenticity, engagement, collaboration, and transferability—but deep down, he knows the mural project would better serve these values.

External Factors

Humans are endlessly creative in the face of external barriers. Is there really no way for him to get that wood to school? If he physically won't be able to teach with three giant boards in his classroom, is there no other place for his students to make the mural? Is there work Henry could eliminate or shorten to make room for the mural in his schedule? If his school lacks the money and resources to make this project work, could he come up with a lower-cost alternative (a sidewalk mural in chalk?) or get a grant? If his principal says no, could he start a conversation with her about the benefits of teaching through the arts?

When people find reasons not to teach by their values, they often see these reasons as external—no time, no money, no space, no support—without realizing or acknowledging how many of these barriers are inside them. It isn't impossible for Henry to get the materials, space, and time he needs for his dinosaur mural, it's just hard.

OVERCOMING BARRIERS TO TEACHING BY YOUR VALUES

Despite the barriers, Henry knows his students would have a great time making the mural and would understand the Mesozoic era better from it than from making booklets. So, he borrows a friend's truck, drives it to the hardware store, and gets help moving the materials. He asks his principal to help him find a place where the mural won't be in anyone's way, and they find a rarely traversed hallway where they set up shop. His colleagues are indeed mad when he does the mural after they all said they didn't want to do it too. He lives with their disapproval. The kids love the project and learn a lot about dinosaurs and about collaboration.

Textbox 1.4 is an exercise to help you identify your own barriers to teaching by your values. If you did the Values Self-Assessment, consider picking a value for which you gave yourself a higher "importance" rating than "consistency" rating. Also consider doing this exercise with a supportive colleague, either by sharing what you wrote with one another or simply talk through your barriers. Hearing about other people's struggles can sometimes give you insight into your own.

If you know which barriers to teaching by your values are internal and which are external, then you also know where you have power and what your choices are. From there, designing values-congruent curriculum will be a continuous process of

IDENTIFYING BARRIERS TO TEACHING BY
YOUR VALUES

Choose a value you're not living by as much as you'd like to be in your
work as an educator.

Write down or talk through everything that stops you from living by that
value in your work. Give yourself time to think through all the types of
barriers and discover what is and isn't in your control.

Self-limiting beliefs you might be stuck in

Examples: *I can't make this work.*

               I don't have the energy.

               I don't know how.

               Teachers like me don't do this.

Uncomfortable feelings you might be avoiding

Examples: *It will be too frustrating/stressful/hard.*

               I'll be embarrassed if it doesn't work out.

               It sounds like too much work.

               I'm afraid my colleagues won't get it.

Ways you might be disregarding what's most important to you

Examples: *It's not worth the time/energy it will take.*

               I'll do it next year.

               No one else is doing it.

               I won't be supported.

External factors

Examples: *There isn't time.*

               I don't have the resources.

               The logistics won't permit it.

               I'm not allowed.

learning how not to be limited by your own self-conceptions, unwillingness to feel unpleasant emotions, and difficulty connecting with your values. It will also become a process of accepting the places where you have no control—places where the barriers are truly external.

If internal barriers show up, you can try a technique called "Yes-and." "Yes-and" comes from improvisational theater and basically consists of shifting your thinking from "Yes, but" (as in, "*Yes*, I could do the mural with my students, *but* my colleagues will get mad") to "Yes, and" (as in, "*Yes*, I could do the mural with my students, *and* my colleagues will get mad"). Yes-anding is one way to accept the inevitable thoughts and feelings that would otherwise keep you from teaching by your values.

If you're interested in learning more strategies for overcoming barriers to teaching (and living) by your values, here are three suggestions for further reading. These books are written for general audiences but are applicable to the challenging and rewarding work teachers do.

- Steven Hayes, *Get out of Your Mind and into Your Life*. This book aims to get people to clarify their values and act in accordance with them in order to live more fulfilling lives. It digs deeply into the ways people avoid values-congruent living and teaches practical strategies for noticing and accepting the thoughts and feelings that limit people.
- Martin Seligman, *Authentic Happiness*. Seligman describes how people can achieve an authentic sense of fulfillment by incorporating their strengths and values into their everyday lives.
- Mihaly Csikszentmihalyi, *Finding Flow*. "Flow" is a state of complete psychological fulfillment, achieved when we're living by our values and challenging our capacities without overstressing them. Csikszentmihalyi explains how to find flow by accepting challenges and overcoming internal barriers to satisfying action.

As you design curriculum in accordance with your values, you might think self-limiting thoughts, be unwilling to feel uncomfortable emotions, or tell stories to steer yourself away from your values. If that happens, you might return to this chapter.

By now, you might be growing more aware of your own values as well as other people's values that shape your work—and you might not be. Plenty of people aren't able to articulate their values the first time they try. Over time, you might begin to pay attention to when you feel vitality and satisfaction in your work, and when you feel frustrated, defensive, overwhelmed, or empty. If none of the exercises in this chapter worked for you, try just noticing your feelings at work and thinking about what values are being served or undermined in those moments.

Designing Curriculum Using Multiple Sets of Values

How do other people's values impact what happens in your classroom?

Schools are complex social institutions with various constituencies: discipline-based departments, grade-level teams, support staff, parent associations, committees, and (let's not forget them) the students. There are also school boards, state and federal leaders, professional associations, and other stakeholders. With all the deeply held and often-conflicting values at work in such a high-stakes environment as a school, it's no wonder that designing curriculum can become a challenging and sometimes emotionally fraught process.

Before you get too far in this process, you'll need to know where you have the autonomy to design and implement curriculum according to your values. This book proceeds from the assumption that content and skill objectives already exist at your school, but there is not necessarily a specified path for getting students to learn the content and skills and for assessing that learning. Designing that path of learning and assessment experiences might be within your creative control, or you might share that control with students, colleagues, and administrators whose values are different from yours.

If you don't know where you have autonomy and where you're expected to be consistent across your department, grade level, or school, then ask. The "Uniformity and Variation in the Curriculum" checklist in table 2.1 is one way you can find out which experiences need to be the same for all classes and which can be different.

Just because you need to do what everyone else does doesn't mean you have no power to suggest changes, and just because you can design your own curriculum doesn't mean you have automatic permission to implement it. Each school has its own process for making decisions to revise the curriculum. You might decide by consensus with your colleagues. You might vote. You might submit proposals to an administrator or committee. In some places, past precedent usually trumps, and in others, new ideas usually go forward. Any process by which curricular decisions get made is itself values laden.

Table 2.1.   Uniformity and Variation in the Curriculum.
In your curriculum, which experiences need to be uniform, where every teacher of this course does the same thing? Which experiences allow for variation depending on the teacher's values?

	Must Be Uniform for All Classes	Would Best Be Uniform for All Classes	Would Best Vary from Class to Class
Content: material students know or understand better or differently than before			
• Big concepts			
• Specific facts, terms, events, etc.			
Skills: actions students perform in a more effective or sophisticated way			
• Discipline-specific skills			
• Cross-disciplinary skills			
Assessments: something that makes visible what students know and are able to do			
• Major assessment tasks			
• Major assessment criteria			
• Skill and knowledge checks			
• Grading system			
Unit Titles			
Essential Questions			
• Use of essential questions			
• Substance of essential questions			
• Wording, number, and order of essential questions			
Resources			
• Books			
• Handouts			
• Special materials			
• Field trips, guest speakers			
Lessons			
• Methods			
• Order of topics			
• Length and pacing of unit			

Since other people's values will undoubtedly impact your curriculum, this chapter will show some examples of how it's possible to design curriculum that reflects multiple and even seemingly conflicting sets of values. It will also offer exercises you can do with students and colleagues to help you see where your values do and don't overlap.

TEACHERS' VALUES VS. STUDENTS' VALUES

Tina has been a beloved P.E. teacher for eighteen years. One of the classes she teaches is fitness for ninth and tenth grade girls who aren't on sports teams. Many of these girls hope to use the class as their way to get skinny. Others have no interest in sports and take the class because it seems like the easiest P.E. option; sometimes these girls don't show up for class at all. Over the years, Tina has gotten great at helping her girls understand their bodies' needs and find manageable yet challenging fitness routines. She's taught them how to use the equipment and how to monitor their progress in terms of repetitions, weights, and times in fitness journals.

Tina's support extends beyond the gym, too. Whenever she sees students in the lunchroom eating only plain pasta or bread, she'll give them a quick lecture on their growing bodies' and brains' need for protein, fat, and other nutrients, and then she'll tell the student to go get some cheese and a banana. One year, some of her students made her a shirt with a picture of cheese and a banana!

Tina represents teachers who have designed an excellent course that doesn't reflect the full scope of their values or their students' values. Perhaps a good way for Tina to focus her course on her values while accounting for those her students bring would be to use a question like *What does "beautiful" look and feel like?* to hook the girls' interest. While continuing to teach fitness skills, Tina could also engage her girls in an inquiry into dominant cultural notions of beauty—perhaps through short class discussions and by talking to women in their families and communities to find out how they conceptualize beauty, health, and wellness.

As long as the students are already monitoring repetitions, weights, and minutes in journals, they could also monitor other health habits like eating, sleeping, and relaxing, as well as their personal ratings of how beautiful and healthy they feel. Tina could help her girls understand how nutritious eating, exercise, and other healthy habits correlate to quality of life.

Since Tina values individualization, she could have each girl design a personal wellness plan that includes diet, exercise, and other elements. The high school girls could even mentor younger girls in designing personalized wellness plans. By bringing a critical examination of beauty into her course, Tina would not only meet her students where they are physically; she'd also meet them where they are in terms of their values.

LEARNING WHAT YOUR STUDENTS VALUE

Finding out what students value can be as simple as giving them opportunities to tell you what matters to them and listening with openness. Some students will easily identify and communicate what's important in their lives. Others, if asked outright what they value, will tell you what they think you want to hear—because they want good grades or are looking to please you—or conversely, they'll give a sarcastic response that doesn't leave them vulnerable. If you do values clarification work with students, they'll need to know you actually care, that you aren't going to judge them, and that they're safe telling the truth.

Students fill out plenty of demographic information and are sometimes asked about goals and interests but not necessarily about their values. Some students will greatly

VALUES CLARIFICATION FOR STUDENTS

When you think about how you want to live your life and the person you want to be, what truly matters to you? Values are how you genuinely want to behave—not because you feel like you're "supposed to" or are trying to make someone else happy, but because they give meaning to your life.

Values aren't goals you can achieve. For example, if you want to get better grades in math, that's a goal. Once you get better grades, you're done. You might set a new goal of maintaining those grades, or getting even better grades, but those are just more goals. If you want to learn all you can from every experience (including every math class), that's a value—a way you can be every day.

Below are questions about areas of life that are important to some people. They might or might not be important to you. Because this is a questionnaire for school, the focus here is on areas of life that relate to school. Some of these areas of life happen outside school; they're here both because they might be important to you and because your school life and your outside-of-school life often affect each other. Please be mindful of your own privacy and your family's if you choose to respond to those questions.

Social: How would you act if you could be the best possible friend? When you think of the kinds of friendships you want in your life, what do those friendships look like?

Civic: Who do you want to be in your community? (You might define "community" as your neighborhood, place of worship, school, or any other group you belong to.) How do you want to contribute? How do you want to relate to the people in your community?

Academic: Try to think beyond grades, scores, and rankings. What kind of student do you want to be on a day-to-day basis? What's important to you as a learner?

Athletic: If you could be the best possible player and teammate, how would you behave?

Artistic: Who do you want to be as an artist (including music, dance, theater, visual arts, etc.)?

Familial: How do you wish you could act toward the members of your family? When you think of the kinds of family relationships you want in your life, what do those relationships look like?

Spiritual: What is important to you in your religious or spiritual life?

Physical: How do you want to take care of your body (like through sleep, relaxation, diet, exercise)?

This exercise is adapted for middle and high school students from Russ Harris (2008b).

appreciate their teacher asking what genuinely and deeply matters to them. Textbox 2.1 is a values clarification exercise adapted for students in grades 6–12. The language is intended to be accessible to middle schoolers without sounding like it's talking down to older students. Feel free to adapt the exercise for your students, or create your own.

An even simpler way to elicit students' values is to ask, "What kind of person do you want to be in . . ." and finish the sentence with different domains of life, like "school," "your family," "your group of friends," "your sports team," or "your neighborhood." Young children could draw pictures or write in journals using these prompts. You can also ask parents or guardians to fill out a values questionnaire on their children's behalf, as long as you acknowledge the risk of getting the adults' values instead of the students'.

If you teach adolescents who are particularly interested in values work, one suggestion for further reading is *Get Out of Your Mind and Into Your Life for Teens* by Joseph Ciarrochi, Louise Hayes, and Ann Bailey. This book helps teenagers clarify their values and use mindfulness to manage the stress, fears, and anxieties that can inhibit values-congruent action.

This all takes precious class time, and it will lead to more work for you if you want to revise your curriculum with students' values in mind. Remember, too, that just as teachers don't always commit to their values or enjoy the efforts associated with that commitment, students won't necessarily work harder or look happier when the curriculum matches their values. You might imagine Tina's girls rolling their eyes when asked to rate their feelings, or groaning, "We have to do homework for gym?"

As with all other aspects of learning, your students will need explicit guidance so they see how their assignments relate to what they think is most important in their lives and become willing to work and struggle. In the best circumstances, though, accounting for students' values in designing the curriculum will pay off when your students learn more deeply and feel more connected to the work they do in your class.

TEACHERS' VALUES VS. OTHER TEACHERS' VALUES

Jill, Vita, and Kenny teach eighth grade English. Their next unit is on Anzia Yezierska's *Bread Givers*, a story set in the 1920s on the Lower East Side, about a working-class Jewish girl who ultimately defies her demanding parents. Jill sees *Bread Givers* as a "girl book" and tries to make sure the boys in her class are engaged. In the past, she's ended the unit with a mock trial where the parents are charged with abuse. Boys and girls alike have loved playing the roles of lawyers and book characters, and the trial format taps into different students' strengths while ensuring everyone analyzes the book closely.

Vita is new to the school this year, and when she read *Bread Givers* she was struck by the ways it perpetuates stereotypes about Jews, the working class, and women. She'd like to have her students write critical essays about how the text appeals to these stereotypes and make visual presentations showing how the media perpetuates similar stereotypes.

Kenny has been teaching at the school for twenty-two years and was the one who initially brought *Bread Givers* into the curriculum, back when eighth graders learned about immigrant populations in their history class. Kenny, who also teaches tenth grade honors English, wants to make sure his eighth graders gain the necessary critical reading and analytical writing skills for high school. His units, including this one, usually end with the students writing essays about a text's theme or symbol.

Kenny, Vita, and Jill have been asked to agree on an approach to this unit so their students all have similar experiences. How can they all teach the same content and skills, and use the same assessments, in a way that will sit right with all three of them?

Vita, Kenny, and Jill could be any group whose members teach the same subject or grade but have very different values in doing so. A good first step for these three eighth grade English teachers would be to clarify and share the values underlying their ideas for the unit. From there, they could work together to craft a unit that satisfies them all. What if the focus was, *How do books both perpetuate and challenge stereotypes?* and the students analyzed the ways *Bread Givers* (and perhaps other texts) does both? Since Vita is passionate about deconstructing the text's stereotypes, perhaps she could find critical readings Jill and Kenny could use and help them plan lessons about stereotype analysis.

Jill seems tuned into how the text tends to appeal more to girls than boys, so perhaps she could design a lesson about books, stereotypes, and the gender of the readers. Since she also values active learning and has found the trial format effective, what if she took the lead in planning a unit assessment were the book itself is put on trial for perpetuating stereotypes? All the eighth graders would then get to do the play-acting and in the process be motivated to analyze the text deeply.

After the trial, the students could write essays analyzing how a particular stereotype works in the text. Kenny could write that assignment to make sure the students are developing the skills they'll need to be successful in high school.

Though Vita, Jill, and Kenny seem to have very different values, they all value close and critical reading, and they all want to position 100 percent of their students to succeed. You might imagine a school where these three teachers would politely go their own ways with the *Bread Givers* unit. That would allow each of them to design a curriculum in accordance with their own values, but their students would lose the benefit of their collective expertise.

VALUES CLARIFICATION FOR GROUPS

If you belong to a team, department, committee, or other group at a school, your shared and unshared values will affect the curriculum you create with and alongside each other. To ensure that work where your values are at stake is effective, you'll need a structure for fearless, generous, and smart communication.

Fearless communication doesn't mean everyone blurts out unfiltered thoughts; it means colleagues can voice their opinions without fearing for their jobs, relationships, or reputations. Generous communication means people give not only their ideas but also overt recognition of each others' skills, passions, and needs. A structure encouraging smart communication is important too; even if teachers have a chance to share ideas, they probably won't think of their most creative ones if they're tired or preoccupied.

One way to find out what your colleagues value would be to invite them to do some values clarification work with you, using the writing exercise in textbox 1.1

TEXTBOX 2.2

VALUES RENDERING FOR GROUPS

For this protocol, each person in the group (e.g., a department or team) brings a text he or she wrote for school—for example, an assignment, course overview, student report, or website. The "text" could even be a photo of each person's classroom or a short video of each person teaching. Ideally, everyone in the group should bring the same *type* of document.

1. The group sits in a circle, and each person passes his or her own document to the left. Now each person reads the colleague's text and underlines phrases that seem particularly striking or important. These don't have to relate to the overall topic or purpose of the text; they only need to seem meaningful or stand out in some way. If the group is using visual texts, each person can circle or highlight parts of the image that seem striking or important. For videos, the members of the group can jot down things they notice. (~5 minutes, depending on the length of the texts)

2. Each reader chooses five underlined parts that seem the most striking or important, and for each, tries to articulate what the person who wrote the text seems to value. (5 minutes) These questions might help:

   - What matters most to your colleague?

   - What does your colleague want for his or her students?

   - What *doesn't* your colleague want his or her students to do? What does this show your colleague *does* care about?

3. Each reader looks over his/her notes and writes a list of things s/he *and* the writer of the text *both* value. (5 minutes)

4. Each person passes the document and the list to the left again. Each person looks over this new document and reads the list of values. The reader marks things on the list that s/he he *also* values. Anything marked on the list is now a value shared by three people in the group. (5 minutes)

(continued)

TEXTBOX 2.2. *(Continued)*

5. Going in a circle, each person shares things on their lists that they marked. A recorder takes notes and reads it back to the group. The group shares any connections and commonalities in what they heard on the list. (10 minutes)

6. Each person gets his or her own document back and looks over the notes on it. The group debriefs the experience of rendering values: (10 minutes)

   - How did it feel to have others read your document for your values?

   - Did you feel misunderstood in any way? Were any values identified in your document that you don't actually hold?

   - What values do you hold that didn't make it to our shared list?

   - What other kinds of documents could this group read in order to make more of our values visible?

or the examples of values in textbox 1.2, and then share out. Another possible exercise is the Values Rendering for Groups protocol (textbox 2.2), where your group uses similar but individually created documents (such as assignments you each wrote) to help make your values more visible to each other and discover shared values.

If you're willing, you can even use conflict as an access point for values. Can you think about a recent conflict within your group as a difference in values? Are there underlying values that are the same? How could you talk to a colleague about your similar and different values? Talking about past conflict can be painful, but it can also be healing and help you find common ground from which to proceed. If nothing else, you and your colleague both *have* values, and acknowledging even this simple point of connection can help.

Yet another way to discover where your group members' values overlap, where they're different, and how to work together is to try the Curriculum Values Orientations protocol (textbox 2.3), which asks you to align yourself to one of four values sets. Most likely, you'll feel that more than one orientation describes you, and you might object to having to choose one. Values clarification is best when it starts as an open-ended process—like the writing and text-rendering exercises in this and the previous chapter—so you don't ignore any values or feel pigeonholed. This orientations activity is a next step for groups.

CURRICULUM VALUES ORIENTATIONS

The curriculum orientations in this protocol are adapted from Michael Stephen Schiro (2013).

1. Read these four orientations and identify the one you feel describes you best. If more than one describes you, choose the one that affects you the most at school right now, particularly if it has led to conflict. (5 minutes)

   - Earth: A school's main job is to prepare students to become effective heads of a household, members of a workforce, and participants in a community. In school, students should learn skills their future employers find important, as well as practical skills they'll need in order to take care of themselves and others. Assessments should be objective measures of how well students can perform specific tasks, allowing teachers to be more efficient in reviewing key skills and content or extending students' skills and knowledge.

   - Fire: A school's main job is to help students become capable of working for social, political, and environmental justice. Students should learn critical thinking, creative problem solving, and communication skills so they can understand societal problems and work with others to solve them. Assessment tasks should have real-world relevance and should measure students' progress as individuals and within the group. Teachers should make sure their students leave school equipped to be caring, empathetic, active, and capable citizens.

   - Air: A school's main job is to teach the knowledge, skills, and mindsets students will need to move forward with an advantage in the world. Teachers need to be experts in their disciplines so they can pass on the understandings and demonstrate the skills students will need to be successful. Assessments should allow teachers to recognize students with the greatest amount of knowledge and skill and to support those with the least. Teachers should make sure their students leave school equipped to be top-performing members of society.

   - Water: Schools should be safe and supportive environments where students can ask questions, make mistakes, and be themselves. Kids

(continued)

TEXTBOX 2.3. *(Continued)*

are naturally curious and need active learning experiences that will stimulate their interests and challenge their intellects. When designing curriculum, teachers should start with the needs of the actual students in the room and make the material rigorous yet accessible and personally meaningful. Assessments are a way to measure each student's individual growth and determine what he or she needs next in order to grow further.

2. Break into groups based the orientations. Discuss these questions, with someone taking notes on the discussion. (15 minutes)

   - What are the benefits of your orientation?

   - What are the limitations of your orientation?

   - Think of a colleague or supervisor you've had conflict with. What orientation do you think s/he would choose? What common ground could you find? How could you discuss your difference? (If a group is larger than four people, form groups of two to three to discuss this question so everyone has a chance to talk.)

3. Each group reports out. (15 minutes)

4. The whole group debriefs the activity, using some or all of the following questions: (10 minutes)

   - What strikes you as you listen to other groups?

   - What do you wish people with other orientations would understand about people with yours?

   - Is it best to work in a group where everyone has the same orientation? All different orientations? Does it matter?

   - How could you get past conflict with those who have different orientations?

   - What contributions do the different orientations make to your personal values?

TEACHERS' VALUES VS. INSTITUTIONAL VALUES

Rashid's principal has mentioned that because sustainability is now part of the school's mission, everyone needs to incorporate this concept into at least one unit. Rashid thinks he's all set: his fifth grade class spends a trimester comparing and contrasting traditional lifestyles of Native American peoples—for example, their homes, foods, clothing, art, and methods of subsistence—and how these relate to their natural environments. The students love the various research and art projects associated with this unit, and they learn about U.S. geography and cultural history in the process.

At a one-on-one meeting, Rashid's principal gently explains how this unit perpetuates the stereotype that Native Americans are remnants of a simpler time when people lived in harmony with the earth and how contemporary Native American groups need to be part of the unit, too. The principal hands Rashid articles about Native American groups protesting fuel pipelines that would disrupt and contaminate their ancestral lands.

Rashid leaves this meeting feeling surprised and overwhelmed. He knows teaching about contemporary Native American environmental activism would satisfy his principal, but he's afraid his students won't understand this material and doesn't see how to integrate it into his unit.

Rashid represents every teacher who's up against an administrative mandate. Some teachers feel pressured to conform immediately to mandates at the expense of more valued curriculum (and their own time). Other teachers tend to see mandates either as repackaged versions of ideas they've seen not work before or as flavor-of-the-month initiatives to be ignored, loudly resisted, or implemented only to the extent necessary to get its champions off their backs so they can "just teach." Is there a middle ground?

In Rashid's case, a workable approach could be to ask his students, *How do groups of people use, abuse, and protect their environments?* Through this question, Rashid could get at how and why Native American cultural groups, and his students themselves, interact with their natural environments in the ways they do. By examining the complexities of the students' own relationships to their natural environments, Rashid could move away from us-vs.-them dichotomies and cultural stereotypes.

Regarding how to bring in contemporary Native American activism in a way that would make sense to young children, Rashid could ask his principal for help inviting in an expert (physically or virtually) so the students could ask questions. The kids might have their own ideas about ways to interact more sustainably with their environments, inspired by historical or contemporary Native American actions.

By bringing in the students' questions and stories, Rashid would be moving toward his value of student engagement. He wouldn't need to give up the activities that work; he'd need to frame them in a way that gets his students to understand how people use, abuse, and protect their environments.

WORKING WITH INSTITUTIONAL VALUES

Institutions aren't people. You can't ask an institution to write down its values. Your school might have a mission statement or a strategic plan, or even a set of stated "core values," but these are subject to different and sometimes contradictory interpretations.

Standards, too, can give rise to all kinds of interpretations of state and national values. On the blog "Living in Dialogue" on Education Week, two guest writers posted about their interpretations of the Common Core's values. The first piece was called

"Common Core Values: Do They Include Authoritarianism?" (Hassard 2012), and a week later came "Values of the Common Core: Equity, Competition, and Collaboration" (Musselwhite 2012). You can't go ask the Common Core what its actual values are; you can only interpret, and these interpretations will be influenced by *your* values.

Sometimes an institution's stated values directly conflict with its operational values. Sonia Nieto and Patty Bode (2008) describe how in many schools where multiculturalism is a stated value, "sincere attempts to decorate bulletin boards with what is thought to be a multicultural perspective end up perpetuating the worst kind of stereotypes. Even where there are serious attempts to develop a truly pluralistic environment . . . the highest academic tracks are overwhelmingly White, the lowest are populated primarily by students of color, and girls are nonexistent or invisible in calculus and physics classes" (45).

Perhaps your institution's values aren't clear, and perhaps some of its stated values conflict with students' or teachers' experiences. Or perhaps your own values are radically different from your institution's. What can you do?

Depending upon how much you value your relationship with your institution and how willing you are to assert your own values, you have several choices. You can leave your school and find a new one with more clearly stated values that better match yours. You can fight or ignore your institution's values and teach by your own (with professional risk to you), or you can ignore your own values and teach by the institution's (with emotional risk to you). If none of these options sound palatable, you can design curriculum that serves institutional values *and* your own.

ACCOUNTING FOR MULTIPLE SETS OF VALUES

A ballpoint pen can serve lots of functions beyond writing. You can use it to poke holes in paper or in the ground. If you remove the ink reservoir and tip, you can use the pen's outer shell as a straw. You can make a whistle out of the cap. One assignment, unit, or course can also serve multiple functions, including the functions you value *and* the functions your students, colleagues, and institution value.

Similarly, a valued purpose—whether it's poking holes in the ground when gardening, or engaging fifth graders in an inquiry—can be fulfilled in many different ways. Though it's easy and normal to get caught up in how much you like the *form* a particular lesson or assignment takes, that assignment or lesson is not the only way to serve the *function* you value. Being flexible about the forms your assignments and lessons (and units and courses) can take will allow you to think of new ways to serve the functions you value as well as those valued by others.

Accounting for multiple sets of values certainly makes the curriculum design process more complicated, but getting other perspectives and ideas can also be rewarding for you and ultimately for your students. Students, administrators, and colleagues can also keep you from changing too much too fast and push you to take your curriculum in a direction you value, too.

3

Using Values to Focus Units

What's most important in teaching this material?

The first year Allison taught *Of Mice and Men*, her seventh graders discussed the animal motif in chapter 1, analyzed setting descriptions in chapter 2, made predictions based on the foreshadowing in chapter 3, evaluated characters' power in chapter 4, and debated George's ethical dilemma in chapters 5 and 6. Then the kids wrote essays, only some of which related to their class discussions. After *Of Mice and Men*, they moved along to other books, and while Allison's lessons and assignments weren't a waste of time, they didn't relate to each other in any intentional way.

Some of Allison's students came to strong insights while reading and writing about *Of Mice and Men*, but their insights were more attributable to their own preexisting reading and thinking skills than anything else. Allison started to notice this and wondered, *If I'm not setting all my students up to reach deep, lasting understandings, can I call what I'm doing "teaching" at all? And if only some of my students are coming to exciting insights, what's everyone else doing?*

THE UNITY OF A UNIT

A unit is a time-bound study of a particular topic: a month on ancient Egypt, a trimester on biomes, a week on Spanish vocabulary related to travel. Units consist of lessons aimed at students learning *content*, material you want them to understand better or differently than before, and *skills*, actions you want them to perform in a more effective or sophisticated way. Skills can be physical (kicking a soccer ball), mental (planning the next play), and social (resolving conflict on the team). Units often include an *assessment*, something that makes visible to you what your students know and are able to do as a result of the unit.

The content and skills in a unit should be interlinked. A unit on ancient Egypt would probably focus on that content, and the students learn skills—reading maps, analyzing artifacts, annotating primary and secondary sources—that help them master and use the content. A unit on solving one-step algebraic equations would probably be skills-focused, and the students learn content—order of operations, the distributive property—that helps them master the skills.

Allison's chunk of content was *Of Mice and Men*, but her unit had no sense of purpose. She wasn't clear on why it was so important for seventh graders in the early twenty-first century to read this particular book. Sure, she could say *Of Mice and Men* was a timeless classic of friendship and loss, but that felt more like an empty tagline than a reflection of her or her students' values. She could also point to reading and writing standards her unit addressed, but surely she could find a way to address the standards in a way that led to a more meaningful outcome.

Linda Booth Sweeney (2001) offers a helpful distinction between a system—where the whole has properties the parts don't—and a heap. Imagine that after a long day at school, you discover that the car you drove to work has been disassembled into a heap of parts. Even though every single part is sitting there in your parking space, the heap won't get you home. A system works for a purpose, but a heap is purposeless. Allison's *Of Mice and Men* unit was a heap. Are your units systems or heaps?

RINGMASTERS AND DROVERS

In *Understanding by Design* (2005, 3), Grant Wiggins and Jay McTighe discuss what they call the "twin sins" of curriculum design: giving students a heap of activities that involve similar topics, and moving students through a huge heap of content.

You can think of the heap-of-activities teacher as a ringmaster: he "introduces the various acts . . . guides the audience through the entertainment experience . . . [and] maintain[s] the smooth flow of the show—or at least an appearance of it" ("Ringmaster (Circus)" 2013). In Allison's *Of Mice and Men* unit, she was a ringmaster, introducing a series of activities, guiding students through them, and maintaining what appeared to be a smooth flow of lessons.

And you can think of the heap-of-content teacher as a drover: she is "contracted to move the mob at a predetermined rate according to the conditions, from a starting point to the destination" ("Drover, Australian" 2013). The "mob" of students might as well be livestock, marching steadily from September to June across miles of content until they reach their destination: the end of the textbook. Perhaps you can remember being a student sitting in the classroom of a drover, patiently chewing your cud, regurgitating when necessary.

As easy as it is to poke fun at these styles of teaching, it doesn't seem helpful or fair to blame teachers when the curriculum looks this way (or to call the product of teachers' hard work a "sin"). Ringmasters and drovers might be complying with expectations like "Keep those kids busy and happy" or "Make sure you cover everything that could show up on the standardized test." If your own teachers were ringmasters and drovers, you might teach the same way until you learn something more effective, or you might rail against the approach that made you miserable by using the other.

What ringmasters and drovers have in common is that both have predefined images of what "teaching" looks like—kids who look busy, or certain material that gets covered—and then aim to make their classes look as much like these images as possible. That's understandable: administrators often base their evaluations on predefined images of "good teaching," popular and professional media contain images of what "good teaching" looks like, and every teacher's experiences as a student will produce images of what teaching should and shouldn't be. Is your goal to make your teaching look a certain way, or is your goal to teach?

Drovers and ringmasters almost certainly value teaching—making deep, meaningful, and lasting learning happen—even if they don't always succeed. Teachers might end up becoming drovers because they value getting lots of knowledge into kids' heads, but does droving effectively increase kids' knowledge in a deep, meaningful, or lasting way? Ringmaster teachers might value engaging and stimulating kids, but is the kids' interest and activity an end in itself, or can it serve deep, meaningful, and lasting learning?

If acting as a ringmaster or drover doesn't necessarily cause learning, what does? Instead of trying to conform to a predefined image of what teaching looks like, you can make deep, meaningful, lasting learning happen by turning the heap of content or activities into a system: a purposeful, cohesive unit.

MAKING TITLES MATTER

One way to begin focusing your unit is to think carefully and critically about what you call it. A unit called "The Rise of Industry" suggests a different series of student experiences and work products than a unit called "Perspectives on the Industrial Revolution," and both suggest a more purposeful unit than "The Industrial Revolution." Some examples of unit titles are:

- Graphing Functions in the Coordinate Plane
- Making a Budget
- Classical Mechanics
- The Human Body's Nutritional Needs
- Choreographing a Tap Dance
- The Art, Poetry, and Politics of the Harlem Renaissance
- Persuading People

- Reinventing *Romeo and Juliet*
- Power Shifts in the Balkans
- Getting around in a French-Speaking Place
- Acing the Advanced Placement Exam
- Redesigning Our Classroom

Many unit titles include a verb and a noun, like "Choreographing a Tap Dance" or "Making a Budget," and some only include nouns, like "The Human Body's Nutritional Needs" and "Power Shifts in the Balkans." The verbs in unit titles name valued processes or skills, and the nouns name valued themes, topics, or work products.

To come up with a useful title for a unit, try brainstorming several possibilities that could work. Choose one that articulates what matters most in your unit and that would help you make decisions about what to teach. Make sure this title will make sense to your students (given their age and characteristics) so they too will understand what the unit is really about.

ESSENTIAL OR VALUED?

Another method for turning the heap into a system is to use essential questions, questions meant to get kids curious and to make meaning out of the material. Wiggins and McTighe define a question as "essential" if it represents "*important* questions that recur throughout all our lives," points to "*core* ideas and inquiries within a discipline," "helps students effectively inquire and make sense of *important* but complicated ideas, knowledge, and know-how," and will "*most engage* a specific and diverse set of learners" (2013, 108–10, emphasis added).

What gets called "important," "core," "central," and "most engaging" depends on values. Within any academic discipline, you'll find at least some consensus around what's central, but these are just statements of what people have said they value. Standards are simply statements of values; their adoption by various states means, in effect, that people in power in these states have agreed that they share the values embedded in the standards. The term "essential questions" can be confusing because there is no natural or intrinsic "essence" of a subject; there are only the values people bring to that subject.

Still, the phrase "essential questions" has permeated the educational lexicon (and yields over a million hits on Google), and "values-congruent learning-stimulating unit-guiding question" just doesn't have the same ring to it.

In this book, the term "essential question" will refer to a question that successfully serves these three functions:

1. *Directing attention to what's most important.* What's "most important" in the unit depends on values: the teacher's, the school's, the community's, and the nation's. Essential questions are a way to show yourself and your students what about the content or process is worth sustained consideration throughout an entire unit.

2. *Piquing the students' genuine curiosity.* Students usually become interested when the question relates to their lived experiences, challenges their beliefs, or addresses a real-world issue that matters to them. The question should also be sufficiently open-ended that students truly (and rightly) believe the teacher isn't playing a game of "guess what I'm thinking." The assumption here is that a teacher needs some sense of what the students value in order to write a good essential question. Chapter 2 describes some ways you can learn what your students value.

3. *Focusing the teacher so s/he knows what doesn't belong in the unit and what does.* As Heidi Hayes Jacobs (2004) puts it, an essential question is "a pragmatic conceptual commitment that frames what you will teach and what you will leave out." These questions represent commitments to focused, purposeful teaching and learning.

Wiggins and McTighe emphasize how essential questions indicate what *doesn't* belong in a unit: an activity or information that doesn't advance the essential inquiry doesn't get included in your unit. Christine Sleeter (2005) discusses how essential questions can also help teachers see what *does* belong: any knowledge that meaningfully advances the inquiry is valuable. That knowledge can come from traditional sources such as the textbook, standards, or canon, and it can also come from the students themselves, their families and neighborhoods, and those cultures and perspectives typically left out of your subject's narrative.

For example, if a chemistry unit uses the essential question *When does pH matter?*, the students might learn as much from their school's maintenance and cafeteria workers as they would from their textbook. If in the P.E. unit described in chapter 2, Tina were to use the essential question, *What does "beautiful" look and feel like?*, her students could interview women of color, lesbian women, and elderly women in their families and communities to find out how they conceptualize beauty, health, and wellness—and those perspectives would be important.

Essential questions thus encourage teachers to engage in what Sleeter calls "the process of retrieving subjugated knowledge"; that is, studying the topic from the perspective of "a sociocultural group whose experiences, perspectives, and/or intellectual work relates to the big idea [of the unit] but is marginalized in it" (91). Guided by your values, you can design questions that remind you to bring traditionally marginalized knowledge into the academic domain.

WHAT ESSENTIAL QUESTIONS SOUND LIKE

To give you a sense of what questions with values-suggesting, interest-piquing, unit-focusing potential sound like, table 3.1 has some examples. Each question has two versions, one for the teacher to use in designing the unit, and one for the students to see posted in the classroom and refer back to when learning.

The question's "student version" tends to have simpler language and fewer words. This is not to say the question needs dumbing down, that it can't include academic

Table 3.1. Examples of Essential Questions

Unit	Essential Question, Teacher Version: • suggests a course for teaching • reflects the values of the learning community	Essential Question, Student Version: • suggests a course for learning • stimulates students' interest and thinking
Persuasive Nonfiction	How do authors attend to the needs of their readers, and how can I attend to my readers' needs when I write a persuasive essay?	How do writers convince their readers?
Simplifying Algebraic Expressions	How does sequence impact outcomes in solving an equation?	Why this order?
Atomic Structure	How do subatomic particles interact to affect the properties of an atom, and how does an atom's properties affect its behavior?	What can atoms do?
Spanish Greetings and Introductions	How can I use social and cultural cues to tell how formal I need to be in addressing someone?	How do I know when to use *tu* and when to use *usted*?
The Constitution	How do checks and balances limit the potential for abuse of power?	Why do we need checks and balances on government power?
Basketball	What techniques and mechanics will determine accuracy in various types of shots?	How can I score when I shoot?
Winter Jazz Concert	How can I control my breath to achieve the desired quality of sound on a wind instrument?	Why do I sound this way?
Painting a Self-Portrait	How can choices of color and shading become acts of self-representation?	What colors represent me?

terms, or that the students' exploration of it shouldn't be nuanced. A good essential question helps students think critically, creatively, and precisely about a topic. At the same time, the question will be more likely to serve its functions of directing students' attention to what's important and stimulating their interest if it's worded in a way the students can access—and that reflects their values too.

The student and teacher versions of each question might not have the exact same meanings, but they don't need to. The questions need to accomplish the same purpose: helping the teacher and students focus on what's most important.

Even with these and many more examples, you might find essential questions difficult to write. You wouldn't be alone: when Wiggins and McTighe were revising *Understanding by Design* for the second edition, they had to do "more painstaking back-and-forths of drafts of [their chapter on essential questions] than were necessary for any other part of the revision" because they "saw an inconsistency between the original account and widespread practice" (vii).

As an exercise, try searching the web for essential questions on a topic you teach. Look for questions that suggest what you think is most important about the topic and that you could imagine stimulating students and focusing a unit. Also look for questions that seem like they'd bore or confuse students, questions that seem too broad or too narrow to focus a whole unit, and questions that direct attention to knowledge and skills that could be helpful but don't suggest what you think matters most.

Many great examples (and helpful nonexamples) of essential questions are in Grant Wiggins and Jay McTighe's book *Essential Questions: Opening Doors to Student Understanding* (2013). Ultimately, it's less important that your question sound like an essential question than that you write one you can use to help you create a unit that works as a meaningful system toward valued outcomes.

FROM VALUES TO ESSENTIAL QUESTIONS

Debbie's quarter-long visual arts course never looks the same way twice. Depending on her students' interests, Debbie might have them use pencil, pastel, or charcoal. If a group works especially well together, she might have them assemble still lifes into one giant composition. If the weather is nice, she might send her spring term students outside to do al fresco paintings. If a model is available, she might teach life drawing. While she always teaches certain skills, like how to do a color study or use negative space, the extent to which Debbie emphasizes them depends on the project and on each student's needs.

Regardless of what happens in any particular quarter, what Debbie most wants her kids to get out of her class is to relearn to see the world, so that instead of using symbols and stereotypes, they can represent the actual shapes, colors, and textures. Debbie was able to articulate these values as essential questions: *How do we see the world through observation rather than through labeling?* and *How do we represent what we see on two-dimensional surfaces?* These questions reflect Debbie's values as an art teacher and make the purpose of her course clear, and she can communicate that purpose to her students.

The teachers from chapter 2 could use these essential questions to reflect the values of all concerned:

- Tina: *What does "beautiful" look and feel like?*
- Rashid: *How do groups of people use, abuse, and protect their environments?*
- Vita, Jill, and Kenny: *How do books both perpetuate and challenge stereotypes?*

Again, even veteran teachers can have trouble writing engaging questions that get at the most important ideas in a discipline and shape the unit. Textbox 3.1 is a protocol designed to help you write essential questions. You'll need an "area of focus"—a topic,

FINDING WHAT'S ESSENTIAL FOR INDIVIDUALS: A PROTOCOL FOR WRITING VALUES-CONGRUENT ESSENTIAL QUESTIONS

This protocol is for teachers who are helping each other generate questions to use in their respective courses. It is not for teachers who are looking to generate questions they'll all use.

Work in a group of at least three. You may wish to add an additional person to serve as a timekeeper/facilitator during this protocol.

Each person will consider a specific area of focus: a topic, resource, issue, skill, or theme.

1. One member of the group (the "presenter") talks about his or her area of focus—the topic, resource, issue, skill, or theme—using the prompts below. The presenter doesn't have to go in any particular order or get to all the prompts. The other members of the group silently listen and take notes. (5 minutes)

   - Why does this matter?
   - Why am I drawn to this?
   - What do I most want my students to get out of this?
   - What do I want my students to be able to do next?
   - How does this connect to the students' lives, their other classes, or their real world?
   - What don't I want to do with this—and how can I turn that on its head?

2. The presenter is silent while the group members say back what they heard, but framed as questions. Try to generate different questions or different versions of the same question. The presenter writes the questions down. (5 minutes)

3. Repeat steps 1 and 2 so each member of the group becomes the presenter (10 minutes per group member).

4. Share some or all of the questions with more colleagues to get feedback. (10 minutes)

   Ways to share include:

- Putting your questions in a shared document for colleagues to comment on
- Posting your questions on the walls and gallery walk, with colleagues adding their comments on sticky notes

Helpful comments from colleagues include:

- Suggestions for rewording the question
- Ideas for teaching using this question
- Connections to their curriculum

resource, issue, skill, or theme for your unit. For example, Tina's area of focus would be fitness.

The most effective way to do this protocol is to work with at least two supportive colleagues who are willing to help you generate questions to use in your course. You could adapt the protocol to use by yourself, but working with others lets you focus on articulating your values for the unit and hand off the work of phrasing them as stimulating, unit-shaping questions to your colleagues. You'll return the favor by writing questions for them—giving you more practice writing essential questions and a chance to hear about what your colleagues do.

Textbox 3.2 is another version of the "Finding What's Essential" protocol, written for groups of teachers expected to use the same essential questions for their units. Vita, Jill, and Kenny—as a group of eighth grade English teachers—could use this protocol to help them come up with a common essential question for their unit on *Bread Givers*. In this version of the protocol, teachers articulate their individual values for a unit, find common ideas, and come up with questions they can all authentically stand behind.

Since writing essential questions is an act of revealing your values, it puts you in a vulnerable space. If you're working with colleagues who teach the same course as you and you're expected to use common questions, try doing some values clarification together (see chapter 2), not only to become aware of each other's values but also to build trust.

Ideally, many small groups of teachers would use these protocols at once so everyone could look at each others' resulting questions, give each other feedback, and learn more about each other's curriculum and values.

After doing one of the protocols, getting feedback on the questions, and revising your wording, you might find yourself with *lots* of questions that flow from your values and sound like they have interest-stimulating and unit-shaping potential. If that

FINDING WHAT'S ESSENTIAL FOR GROUPS:
A PROTOCOL FOR WRITING VALUES-
CONGRUENT ESSENTIAL QUESTIONS

This protocol is for teachers who are looking to generate questions they'll all use.

Work in a group of at least three. You may wish to add an additional person to serve as a timekeeper/facilitator during this protocol.

The group will consider a common area of focus: a topic, resource, issue, skill, or theme.

1. Consider your area of focus—the topic, resource, issue, skill, or theme— and write for five full minutes without stopping, using the prompts below. You don't have to go in any particular order or get to all the prompts; choose the ones where you have something to say. The point isn't to write beautifully or say the "right" thing but to find your values.

   - Why does this matter?
   - Why am I drawn to this?
   - What do I most want my students to get out of this?
   - What do I want my students to be able to do next?
   - How does this connect to the students' lives, their other classes, or their real world?
   - What don't I want to do with this—and how can I turn that on its head?

2. Each member of the group shares what he or she wrote while the others listen and take notes. (5 minutes per group member)

3. All members of the group review their notes and look for connections and commonalities among the responses. (5 minutes)

4. Members of the group say back some of the connections and commonalities, but framed as questions. Try to generate different questions or different versions of the same question. A scribe writes the questions down. (5 minutes)

5. Share some or all of the questions with more colleagues to get feedback. (10 minutes)

Ways to share include:

- Putting your questions in a shared document for colleagues to comment on
- Posting your questions on the walls and gallery walk, with colleagues adding their comments on sticky notes

Helpful comments from colleagues include:

- Suggestions for rewording the question
- Ideas for teaching using this question
- Connections to their curriculum

happens, try choosing one or two, and no more than three, essential questions to use for your unit. There's no "right" number of essential questions, but if the questions are to help you focus your unit, you're probably better off limiting the number of questions and going into greater depth when using each one.

If you use titles *and* essential questions, you might discover that one works better than the other at articulating what's most important, piquing student interest, and focusing you on what does and doesn't belong in the unit—or you might find that both are helpful, especially if you use more than one question in a single unit. Titles can be more concrete reminders to students of what the unit is really about, while essential questions capture multiple valued outcomes and are reminders that knowledge construction comes from a process of inquiry.

Now that you have essential questions, a title, or both, to keep you focused on what's important, you're ready to create a unit that works as a system.

4

Organizing Lessons in a Values-Congruent Unit

How will you move your students toward a deeper understanding of the important concepts?

While essential questions are helpful tools, they don't provide a lesson-by-lesson blueprint for the unit. You still need to figure out what lessons to teach and in what order so your students will reach the deep and lasting understandings you value, and you also need to decide how to assess their understandings. This chapter deals with generating ideas for student learning experiences and organizing these lessons into a unit, and the next chapter is about assessment.

GATHERING

Creating a unit can begin the same way as creating anything else, as an exploratory and generative process, akin to collecting twigs and leaves that might later be made into a nature collage, or to shooting lots of street footage that might later be used in a documentary film. Try to find or produce lots of material—more than you'll end up using in the finished unit. Like in filmmaking and collaging, you'll need to be selective and critical later, choosing the bits that will work best and structuring them in a coherent way.

Unit design thus begins with lots of research: reviewing standards and curriculum guides, gathering print and visual texts, finding local field trip opportunities and experts (including the students themselves and their families), and collecting ideas for activities that could build more sophisticated understanding.

Sometimes, the materials you find won't be quite right for your students. A first grade teacher who's planning a bird study might find technical guidebooks written for a much more sophisticated reader and simple picture books that lack the detail he wants his students to learn. A middle school history teacher looking for films about the Vietnam War might find them all too graphic or too long to use in class. You can adapt these sorts of materials for your students, use them as resources as you make original materials, or perhaps not use them at all.

The research you do in the early stages of unit design can also be accidental: an article or picture in your social media feed, a show or commercial on TV, a conversation with a friend, or an outing with your family will give you an idea for a lesson. As an exercise, try skimming a general-interest website or channel-surfing your TV while asking yourself for each article or show, "How could this connect to my current unit?"

Again, the point of finding all this material is not to use it indiscriminately; that would create a heap of lessons and not a meaningful system. The point is to let yourself invent new possibilities that you can later shape into a unit. Table 4.1 shows an example of the results of all this gathering: lists of potential topics, activities, and resources for a science unit on the Chesapeake Bay Watershed.

A fun way to get even more ideas during this generative stage of unit design is to work with a group of colleagues. Textbox 4.1 is a protocol you can use with any size group of teachers (though more people means more ideas). Working with teachers of your subject means you'll benefit from their expertise, and working with teachers of all different subjects could be a way to get to know each other's curriculum, gain fresh perspectives on your own, and discover cross-disciplinary connections.

CHOOSING WHAT TO INCLUDE—AND WHAT TO LET GO

When you're pulling together ideas for a unit, there might be a moment when you feel overwhelmed by all the stuff you've amassed, or even depressed because you know you can't do it all. Try to appreciate that moment, because it signals that you're serving your values: the prospect of trimming down the unit might sound hard because you've gathered so many materials and activities you think are worthwhile. Sometimes, the biggest challenge in designing curriculum is letting go of things you like.

For example, imagine that a beloved assignment in seventh grade English involves reinterpreting poems in different artistic media. Kids make paintings, dances, and videos based on poems. One student bakes a cake with each layer a different color and flavor to represent a corresponding stanza of Edgar Allan Poe's "Annabel Lee." Over the years, the teacher redesigns the unit using essential question, *What techniques do poets use, and how can I use them too?* The students learn to use literary devices purposefully in their own poems, but the fun art activity no longer fits. The teacher feels a little sad: no more "Annabel Lee" cakes.

If you experience a feeling of loss like that, it's helpful to notice and name it, because if you can articulate what values you're serving through the eliminated topic or activity, then you can reincorporate those values in other ways. If the poetry teacher values the creativity, artistry, individual choice, and multimodal expression students brought to the poetry art project, she can make sure to serve those values in other ways, within the poetry unit and beyond.

Table 4.1. Topic, Activity, and Resource Lists for a Unit
Unit Title: The Chesapeake Bay Watershed
Essential Question: *What is a watershed, and how am I part of one?*

Possible Topics
- Water cycles
  evaporation, sublimation, and transpiration
  condensation, precipitation, and infiltration
  freshwater and saltwater bodies
  groundwater, springs, streamflow, snowmelt,
  runoff
- How watersheds work
- Animal and plant life in the watershed
  keystone species
  indicator species
  mutualisms
  natives vs. invasives
  economically and culturally significant species
- Sources of pollution
  point sources
  runoff of nutrients, pesticides, and sediment
  from urban, suburban, and rural areas
- Natural watershed filtration systems
  wetlands
  riparian buffers
- Water quality indicators
  macroinvertebrates
  pH
  turbidity
- Relationship between natural and cultural
  histories of the bay
- Management of the watershed
  storm surge
  wastewater treatment
  restoration projects
- Ways to use the watershed responsibly

Possible Learning Activities
- Identifying our connections to the watershed
- Making a contour map of the watershed
- Cataloguing animals and plants of the
  watershed
- Game on how water is filtered naturally
- Home audits of water usage and household
  hazardous waste
- Simulation on how the river got polluted
- Experiment: How clean is our water?
- Simulation of a Chesapeake Bay advisory
  panel that debates ecological and economic
  costs and benefits of different kinds of land
  use

Possible Print, Online, and Visual Texts
- Chesapeake Bay Foundation, Chesapeake Bay
  Program, Anacostia Watershed Society, and
  EPA websites
- Chesapeake Explorer app
- *Essential Atlas of Ecology*
- Tom Horton, *Bay Country*
- Larry Gonick and Alice Outwater, *A Cartoon
  Guide to the Environment*
- Alice Outwater, *Water: A Natural History*
- guidebooks to the Bay region
- maps of the Bay region

Possible Field Trips, Speakers, and Interviewees
- Claggett Farm
- Blue Plains Advanced Wastewater Treatment
  Plant
- Smith Island
- food workers
- landscapers

If you reach that moment where you feel overwhelmed, depressed, exhausted, or just ready to stop, let your essential questions (or unit titles) serve their gatekeeper function. Of everything you've brainstormed, which ones would *best* move your students toward the deeper understandings you value? Do any of the activities, materials, or topics you think you should eliminate make you feel a sense of loss? What values are they serving, and how can you serve those same values in other ways?

TEXTBOX 4.1

VALUES-GUIDED BRAINSTORMING PROTOCOL

For this protocol, each teacher needs at least one essential question for a unit. The group also needs sticky notes in four different colors.

1. Each teacher writes an essential question on a sheet of paper and posts the paper on the wall.

2. Everyone takes sticky notes in four different colors (e.g., pink, yellow, green, and blue).

3. Everyone walks around the room and reads each other's essential questions. They put sticky notes around the questions with suggestions for the unit. Each color represents a different category:

   - Pink—Topics: *What topics could be part of this unit?*

   - Yellow—Activities: *What activities could students do in this unit?*

   - Green—Media Resources: *What could students read or view as part of this unit? Consider all types of print and online texts: books, articles, poems, data sets, images, videos, etc.*

   - Blue—People and Places: *Who could speak to students, or where could the students go, in order to learn? Consider experts and locations of all kinds, including those in the students' families and communities.*

4. After a reasonable length of time, everyone pulls down his or her questions and continues to brainstorm for his or her own units.

As you're deciding how to define the scope of your unit—what you'll include and what you'll leave out—you'll also need to think about sequencing your lessons in a way that will help your students reach valued understandings.

BEGINNING A UNIT WITH WHAT'S FAMILIAR

Tracey Tokuhama-Espinosa (2010) explains how people learn new ideas by linking them to familiar ones: "The brain receives information through the senses, and this information is constantly compared with what it already knows. . . . The brain then makes predictions about what it expects based on past experiences" (212). The lessons at the beginning of a unit should therefore help students connect what they already know—from previous school-based learning, their home and community experiences, or any local current events—to what they'll be learning in the unit.

Elliott's seventh graders begin the year with a unit on the basics of geography, using the essential question, *How does where you live influence how you live?* (McTighe and Wiggins 2013, 5). For the unit's first lesson, Elliott asks a more specific version: *How does where you learn influence how you learn?* Some students examine a study room and conclude that the big tables are conducive to group work but make individual work difficult. Others observe and interview younger kids on the playground to see how its structures promote different decision-making capacities. The students then have discussions and write reflections about ways location affects learning.

One might imagine alternative lessons like *How does where we eat influence how we eat?* or *How does where we socialize influence how we socialize?* Once students use familiar experiences to understand how their own physical location affects their daily behaviors, they can begin constructing a larger idea of how physical geography impacts cultural life. Then, they can apply their understandings to less familiar situations in future units, such as how the Fertile Crescent influenced cultural development in Mesopotamia.

Beginning with "what's familiar" is tricky because each student comes in with a different set of experiences. A student will approach a unit on farming differently depending on whether he's lived on a farm, visited a farm, or read about farms—and also depending on the types of farms he's encountered. Asking students to share their experiences with farms exposes the diversity of background knowledge in the room, giving students with greater knowledge a chance to be the experts.

On the other hand, some students don't want to be class experts, especially if that expertise puts them at risk of being associated with a stereotype. For example, a girl who grew up on a farm and now lives in the Bronx might be afraid of being perceived as a "hick" by her classmates. Stereotype threat is a phenomenon where people who feel they're at risk of being associated with a negative stereotype about their group tend to underperform, distance themselves from the stereotyped group they belong to, and disengage from whatever domain is making the stereotype more salient (Stroessner and Good 2009).

Since you don't want your students to underperform or to dissociate themselves from their own groups or from your class, you need to be careful when beginning with "what's familiar." Asking students questions instead of making assumptions about their backgrounds is always a good idea, and if you do uncover background expertise, it helps to pre-talk with students and their families to make sure they're comfortable sharing their knowledge with their classmates.

When Elliott began his Basics of Geography unit with an exploration of the school, he turned the students' shared environment into a topic worth studying and gave everyone a meaningful entry point into the geography unit. Other ways to connect a unit to students' lives include starting with an experiential exercise or field trip, inviting in a speaker from the community, building upon a project from the previous unit, or asking students to interview members of their families.

Bringing the students' lives into the classroom at the beginning of a unit shows them right up front that their own experiences are worthy of academic inquiry and that their new learning will be a purposeful, meaningful expansion of what they already know. In other words, beginning with students' lives can do more than simply "activate prior knowledge." It can activate their values as well.

INTRODUCING NEW MATERIAL

Once students have a context for learning, they're ready to take in new information, learn new skills, and make new meaning. During these lessons, students could analyze documents and images, play games, participate in discussions and written conversations, conduct experiments, collect data, examine artifacts or make their own—in short, interact with the material in ways that allow them to process it deeply.

Within a unit, interlinked lessons advance students' understanding in much the same way that the chapters in a novel or episodes in a TV series each add to the progression of the story. You might give your lessons their own titles (just as chapters and TV shows often have titles), or you might write an aim for each lesson that builds on the previous lesson's aim.

You might even think of each lesson as answering a subsidiary question of the unit's essential question. When Elliott created his lesson on *How does where you learn influence how you learn?*, he simply substituted the more specific word "learn" for the general "live" in the essential question *How does where you live influence how you live?* and elegantly scaled down a unit-based question into something students could access in a single lesson and preparing them for more abstract understandings later in the unit.

Subsidiary questions, aims, and titles can serve the same purposes for individual lessons that essential questions serve for units: they show which topics matter most, get your students interested, and help you see what to put into your lessons and what to leave out. If you write out your lesson-specific questions, aims, or titles as a series, you can help yourself and your students see how the lessons create a meaningful progression towards a larger understanding. Textbox 4.2 shows a series of lesson-focusing questions for a poetry unit.

CHOOSING INSTRUCTIONAL METHODS

Choosing instructional methods is another values-laden aspect of unit design. Your purpose, causing students to learn new material, can be fulfilled through many different instructional activities, and one activity can serve many purposes. As you plan your unit, consider how you're balancing different kinds of lessons:

- Students receiving vs. constructing information
- Types of activities, such as discussions, simulations, games, labs, writing-to-think practices, etc.

TEXTBOX 4.2

A SERIES OF LESSON-FOCUSING QUESTIONS

Essential Question: *What techniques do poets use, and how can I use them too?*

Lessons:

1. Why do poets write poems?

2. What kinds of topics do poets write about?

3. Why must poets become experts on their topics?

4. How do I become an expert on my topic?

5. Why do poets use repetition?

6. How do I write a poem that uses repetition?

7. Why do poets use sound devices?

8. How do I write a poem that uses sound devices?

9. Why do poets use juxtaposition?

10. How do I write a poem that uses juxtaposition?

11. Why do poets use metaphor?

12. How do I write a poem that uses metaphor?

13. How can add more specific imagery to my poems?

14. How do I write a meaningful introduction to my poetry collection?

15. What kinds of editing does my poetry collection need?

- Taking in information through reading, listening, watching, or experiencing
- Communicating knowledge through writing, speaking, art, or movement
- "Schooly" vs. real-world work
- Individual vs. cooperative learning

You'll probably think of other balances specific to your subject and grade level. The "right" balance depends on values, and balance itself is a value. In choosing techniques, you'll undoubtedly also consider your students' characteristics and needs, your unit topic, your school's resources, and your time frame. When deciding on an instructional method for a particular lesson, you can always ask yourself, "How will this help move my students toward a deep understanding of the valued concepts and processes?"

A fuller discussion of instructional techniques and lesson planning is beyond the scope of this book. For guidance on how to teach almost any topic imaginable—

whether it's dinosaurs, digital photography, or document analysis—you'll probably be able to find a book that goes into great depth about it. Here are a few books with instructional techniques that can be adapted for lots of different subjects and students:

- Thomas Lasley, Thomas Matczynski, and James Rowley, *Instructional Models: Strategies for Teaching in a Diverse Society.* This textbook describes various methods of getting students to understand new concepts.
- Elizabeth Barkley, K. Patricia Cross, and Claire Howell, *Collaborative Learning Techniques.* Though this text is written for college faculty, the techniques it describes are adaptable for students of all ages. These techniques are designed to structure student groups to help students have discussions, teach each other, solve problems, organize information, and create a written product—always with the end goal of learning new content.
- Ron Ritchhart, Mark Church, and Karin Morrison. *Making Thinking Visible.* The authors describe various "thinking routines," or ways to explore new content, organize ideas about it, and analyze it more deeply.
- Pérsida Himmele and William Himmele, *Total Participation Techniques: Making Every Student an Active Learner.* The authors describe dozens of teaching techniques that get students more involved, and they explain how to adapt these techniques for different age levels and subjects.
- Teresa Vilardi and Mary Chang, *Writing-Based Teaching.* From the Bard College Institute of Writing and Thinking, this book contains essays about writing to think, or practices where students write to explore and deepen their thinking about any topic.

CREATING MEANINGFUL CONTEXTS FOR STUDENT WORK

If you value students understanding a particular set of ideas or skills, then you probably also value their holding onto their understandings over time. You might be tempted to drill so your students can practice what they're learning, but practice needs to be in a meaningful context.

Steve Graham and Dolores Perin (2007) found that grammar instruction isolated from writing actually makes students' writing *worse*. Daryl Siedentop, Peter Hastie, and Hans Van Der Mars (2004) noticed that too many P.E. units were "dominated by isolated skill drills" and that instead of becoming better sport players, "many students were left frustrated or just plain bored" (2). Eugene Geist (2010) describes math classrooms when teachers overfocus on skill drills: "Instead of helping children develop fluency at computation and become more efficient at problem solving, these policies have produced students that rely more on rote memorization and have increased the level of anxiety in young children" (25). Out-of-context drills don't help students learn.

Projects

One way to create a context for deeper learning is to design a project. Projects are opportunities for students to learn skills and content *you* value through the process of making something *they* value. Students might learn how to use precise language, vivid imagery, and poetic devices—skills their teacher values—while writing poems on a topic of personal importance and creating meaning that matters to them. Projects can also help students develop interdisciplinary life skills like collaboration, creative problem solving, and resilience.

Calling work a "project" doesn't guarantee that students will learn valued content and skills while doing it. Sylvia Martinez and Gary Stager (2013) lament that when teachers call an assignment a "project," they often mean "any activity that is not worksheet-based or that takes longer than a 42-minute class period" (58). A good project doesn't simply take more time; it gives teachers and students a goal for the unit. All activities move students toward successfully completing the project, and students pick up content and skills they need in context of "work that is substantial, shareable, and personally meaningful" (57). The project's outcome usually serves as a unit assessment.

Cycles of Instruction, Practice, and Application

Another way to create a context for skill development is to cycle students through individualized instruction, cooperative practice, and low-stakes application. During Jeff and Tony's basketball unit, each class period begins with individual practice of skills such as dribbling and shooting layups. The students form teams, with student-coaches designing cooperative practice routines, like having their team members take turns dribbling the ball to the basket and shooting a layup, with a partner catching the ball and passing it to the next player. After practices, student teams apply these skills in short games.

Learning any skill set will present opportunities to take on different roles, such as writer and peer reviewer of an essay, artist and critic of a portrait, or speaker and listener of a target language. Giving each student opportunities to experience multiple roles will only serve to expand their skill set and gain a deeper sense of why those skills are important.

In the basketball unit, student roles could include coach, equipment manager, and scorekeeper. Jeff and Tony's students rotate their roles regularly so they all get to experience the game from different perspectives. The kids also learn skills in organization, materials management, decision making, and leadership. Students need time to learn skills associated with their roles so they'll be successful, so Jeff and Tony hold regular meetings with groups of students in each role; for example, they'd hold coaches' meetings to see how team practice sessions are going and to give tips for running more inclusive and rigorous practices.

REGULARLY RETURNING TO WHAT MATTERS

Without regular and explicit returns to the essential question, students can easily forget the bigger purpose of the unit and think the point is to do cute activities or memorize little bits of information. (Indeed, that probably *has* been the point of at least some of their schooling.) If Elliott hadn't framed his *How does where we learn affect how we learn?* lesson within the larger context of connecting physical and cultural geography, his students might have wondered why they had to run around campus taking notes about their school when the whole point of the course was to learn about *other* places.

Returning to the essential question can be as simple as posting it on the classroom wall and briefly explaining how each day's lesson connects to it. Students can also discuss in class or through writing how particular lessons, or sets of lessons, relate to the question.

Siedentop et al. point out that learning a sport "creates the context within which students can learn valuable personal and social lessons" about cooperation, mutual support, fair participation, and personal responsibility, but that it's "up to the teacher and students, working together, to take advantage of the opportunities the context provides" (2004, 93). A teacher—of P.E. or any subject—who values, say, creating a supportive atmosphere might have her students rate each other's supportiveness, write reflections on how supportively they behaved toward their classmates, or simply take a moment to think about things they did that day to show support.

Reflection on skills related to any valued domain can help students retain those skills and use them within and beyond the class.

USING THE CALENDAR

Deciding what will and won't go into a unit requires looking at the school calendar. *How many lessons should I teach in this unit? Thanksgiving is coming up, so should I try to end the unit before the break or start up again after break? Does that mean I'll have to spend Christmas break grading? I guess I can live with that. OK, so fifteen class periods for the unit? Will that be enough? Oh wait—my first period class won't meet next Monday because of the special assembly. Should I try to fit the unit into fourteen class periods for that group? What do I cut? Oh, and what if there's a snow day . . .*

Given how complicated and unpredictable school schedules and calendars can be, it's no wonder many teachers don't use them very much in their unit planning. But if you don't use the calendar, you might run into problems.

If you teach multiple sections of the same course, you might end up with one group way ahead of another. If you add days to a unit because your students need more time to do a project or study before an exam, then later in the year you might have to plow through whatever material is left that might appear on a standardized test. Or perhaps you don't get to certain material at all, and the kids simply don't learn it. Perhaps you've heard stories of classes that ended in June with students halfway through a book—or perhaps you've taught those classes!

It's not *bad* to allow a unit to go on longer than you'd initially planned, especially if your students are fascinated by the topic or if they need more time to gain valued knowledge or skills. But the school calendar, with its many interruptions and pressures, has a nasty way of taking control of your course unless you take control first. Instead of allowing whichever units happen to come earliest in the year to go on forever and then having to shortchange or altogether lop off the later units, you can use your school calendar to plan your year.

When you use the calendar, you're making values decisions: how should you spend the time you have in order to reach outcomes that matter to you, your students, and your school? You don't have to decide in September on the exact date when your April rainforest unit will begin, but mapping out the approximate length of each unit will help you ensure that the rainforest unit happens at all. You might also serve your values by building some unstructured time into each unit so your students have opportunities to pursue their own ideas and direct their own learning, and so you have time to capitalize on "teachable moments."

MAKING A LESSON CALENDAR

Again, if you want your students to develop a deeper understanding of valued concepts or processes, then the lessons within your unit need to build toward that understanding. As you organize your unit into a series of lessons, some questions to consider are:

- How many days will you devote to this unit?
- How much time will you spend on the different parts of the unit?
- In what order will you teach different topics?
- How will you build in regular opportunities to return to the essential question so the students can reflect upon what they've learned?
- When will you assess the students' understanding?

Tables 4.2 and 4.3 show unit calendars for the science unit on the Chesapeake Bay Watershed and for a math unit on Graphing Functions in the Coordinate Plane. Each calendar reflects a particular set of decisions about how to structure the unit in a way that will help the students reach valued understandings.

Table 4.2. Unit Calendar: Graphing Functions in the Coordinate Plane

Essential Question(s): *How can I tell if there's a functional relationship, and why does it matter?*

Class #	Class	Homework
1	Introduce the unit and assign groups. *Minilesson:* Plotting points on the coordinate plane using ordered pairs. *Small group work: Battleship*-style game on plotting points.	Do the problem set on plotting points that your group leader selected.
2	Homework review in groups. *Minilesson:* Graphing data sets in the coordinate plane. *Small group work:* Worksheet on graphing data sets.	Do the problem set on graphing data sets that your group leader selected.
3	Homework review in groups. *Minilesson:* Determining whether a graph shows a correlation, a function, or neither; and whether a table shows a correlation, a function, or neither. *Small group work:* Matching game to associate graphs, tables, and equations.	Do the problem set on determining whether tables and graphs show correlations, functions, or neither that your group leader selected.
4	Homework review in groups. *Minilesson:* Describing functions verbally and algebraically in slope-intercept form. *Small group work:* Worksheet on writing formulas for functions and describing those functions verbally.	Do the problem set on describing functions that your group leader selected.
5	Homework review in groups. *Small group work:* Review problem sets determined by group leaders.	Do the review problem set that your group leader selected.
6	Show a model of the graphing project. Give examples of good research questions: • Do the number of hours of sleep we get relate to how we do on quizzes? • Does the amount of money we spend on clothes relate to how we feel about ourselves? • Is there a relationship between the amount of time we spend with friends and how we feel? Discuss how to choose a good research question and how to do research using surveys or interviews. Small groups choose their questions and create research plans where everyone has an equal role.	Do the research for your graphing project.

7	Groups make their tables, scatter plot graphs, best-fit lines, and equations in slope-intercept form.	(As needed—determined by group leaders.)
8	Review of presentation skills. Groups plan their presentations.	Rehearse your part of your group's presentation.
9	Groups present their graphs to each other. Everyone does a gallery walk, leaving sticky notes on each others' posters, commenting with their reactions to the data. Class discussion: Why do you think your graphs turned out to be functions, correlations, or neither? Why are most graphs correlations, not functions? What would need to be true for the graphs to be functions? How can we use what we see on these graphs to help us make decisions about our behaviors? What other information would we want to know?	Study for the test.
10	Micro-lesson on making an eye-catching poster. Groups use the comments and discussion to help them write an easy-to-understand description of their findings. They turn their graphs and descriptions into mini-posters.	Study for the test.
11	Groups put up their mini-posters in strategic places around the school (e.g., the guidance office, the cafeteria, the bathroom) to raise awareness about the issues in the posters. Groups have a final study session for the test.	Study for tomorrow's test.
12	Test: Graphing Functions in the Coordinate Plane	Write a paragraph self-assessing your skills in math, research, and group membership. Write a thank-you note to a member of your workgroup in which you express appreciation for his or her specific contributions to the project.

Table 4.3. Unit Calendar: The Chesapeake Bay Watershed

Essential Question(s): *What is a watershed, and how am I part of one?*

Class #	Class	Homework
1	Field Trip to Claggett Farm	Respond to the questions on the "Why Claggett Farm" worksheet.
2	How does the water cycle work?	Label the water cycle diagram.
3	How does a watershed work? Activity: Making a Contour Map	Continue working on your part of the class contour map.
4	How does the Chesapeake Bay Watershed work? Contour Maps Work Period	Finish your part of the class contour map.
5	How does the Chesapeake Bay Watershed work? Finish Contour Maps	Choose five terms from the "Bay Vocabulary" list. For each, write how that term is connected to the Bay and how it's connected to you.
6	How do people use land in the Chesapeake Bay Watershed? Activity: Understanding Land Use	For your assigned land use, (1) explain who benefits from this type of land use and how, (2) explain who suffers because of this type of land use and how, and (3) give one specific suggestion for how to meet our needs for this type of land use but cause less harm.
7	What species live in the Chesapeake Bay Watershed? Why should we care about them? Activity: Cataloguing the Bay	Illustrate the pages of your animal and plant life guidebook that we worked on in today's class.
8	What species live in the Chesapeake Bay Watershed? Why should we care about them? Finish Activity: Cataloging the Bay	Read *Essential Atlas of Ecology*, p. 76–77, 87.
9	How are "natural" and "human" land uses connected? Activity: Urban Nature Walk	Using today's nature walk as a model, find a plant or animal near your home and (1) use your scientific drawing skills to sketch it, (2) write about its behavior, and (3) write about how you're connected to it in any way.
10	What does it mean for the Chesapeake Bay Watershed to be healthy? Game: Chesapeake Bay Ecology	Read *Essential Atlas of Ecology*, p. 22–29
12	What does it mean for the Chesapeake Bay Watershed to be healthy? Activity: Who Polluted the Bay?	Read *Essential Atlas of Ecology*, p. 52–59.

Day	Topic	Homework
13	What are the causes and effects of different types of pollution? Point Source Pollution	Read the article about nutrient runoff.
14	What are the causes and effects of different types of pollution? Nutrient Runoff	Read the article about types of toxic runoff.
15	What are the causes and effects of different types of pollution? Toxic Runoff	Do the household hazardous waste survey.
16	What are the causes and effects of different types of pollution? Sediment Runoff	Read Essential Atlas of Ecology, p. 60–67, and the article on sources of air pollution.
17	What are the causes and effects of different types of pollution? Connecting Air Pollution to Water Pollution	Read Essential Atlas of Ecology, p. 80–93.
18	How do natural systems clean our water? Skits: Forest and Wetland Buffers	In preparation for our trip to the Blue Plains Advanced Wastewater Treatment Plant, do the water treatment worksheet.
19	How do we clean our water? Blue Plains field trip	Read the excerpt from Tom Horton's "Potomac: The Nation's Sewage Plant" and then answer the critical thinking questions on Blue Plains.
20	Can we make our drinking water cleaner? Activity: Making a Water Filter	Prepare for tomorrow's lab by reading about water quality indicators.
21	How clean is our water? Lab: Using Water Quality Indicators	Write up the following sections of a lab report for today's lab: purpose, hypothesis, materials, procedure, observations.
22	How clean is our water? Finish Water Quality Lab	Finish writing your lab report: complete the procedure and observations sections, and write a discussion section.
23	How can we reduce our impact on the watershed? Tip Sheets for the Community	Continue working on your tip sheet.
24	How can we reduce our impact on the watershed? Finish Tip Sheets	Distribute your group's tip sheet to people from at least five different households in the Chesapeake Bay Watershed.
25	What is a watershed, and how am I part of one? Personal Commitment Statements	Complete your twenty-four-hour goal for reducing your impact on the Chesapeake Bay Watershed.

MAKING ADJUSTMENTS

Writing a calendar doesn't mean you need to follow it as if it were a set of step-by-step directions for how to put together a bookcase. You might get better ideas. Your students might express interest in a particular topic. You might talk to a colleague about how a lesson just went, and she'll have an idea for what you can do next. A relevant exhibit might open at an art museum. The author of a text you've been using might suddenly be discovered to have made up half his facts. A hurricane might force your school to close for over a week. You might get an idea for a follow-up unit you now want to squeeze in before spring break.

With all that can happen, a unit plan isn't limiting; it's helpful. The movie *Apollo 13* has a scene when the crew has to reenter the earth's atmosphere at the proper angle, but their navigation computer is turned off to save power. The astronauts keep the moon in the window to help them maintain their course. A unit plan serves this navigating function: It reminds you of decisions you've made based on your values, helps you decide whether your inevitable adjustments will keep your unit heading in a valued direction, and shows you how to course-correct when you stray.

Values-Congruent Assessments

What product or performance will make it visible that your students understand the important concepts?

An assessment is anything that makes it possible for you to see and measure what students know and can do. Nancy, a choral music teacher, would like to see whether her students understand musical notation. She could give a written quiz where her students label notes on a staff, she could play a short piece and have the students transcribe it in musical notation, she could have each student write a description of musical notation, or she could give the students pieces of sheet music and have them sight-sing (that is, sing the correct notes when looking at the sheet music for the first time).

Your purpose—making your students' understanding visible—can always be accomplished through many different assessment tasks, and one task can serve many purposes. If Nancy ends up asking her students to sight-sing a piece of music, she might be serving some or all of these purposes:

- seeing how well her students understand musical notation
- giving them practice doing a real-world task that actual musicians do
- enabling the students to hear each other
- allowing her to give grades on the spot so she won't have to bring any work home

Most of these values relate to the students' learning. Nancy is also serving values related to personal well-being by limiting the amount of work she has to take home. There's certainly nothing wrong with taking care of yourself, as long as you're also acting in accordance with your most deeply held values as a teacher.

Nancy's colleague in the music department, Hector, gives a written quiz where students label notes on a staff. Even though the form of assessment is different, one of the functions is the same:

- seeing how well his students understand musical notation
- providing a tangible record of progress that the students can store and access easily
- enabling his students to self-assess with an answer key
- allowing him to grade the quizzes at home when he can concentrate and be more accurate

You might have strong feelings about which of these is the best assessment tool, but neither is inherently the "right" one. A good assessment successfully makes visible to you that your students have learned the valued concepts and skills, so the "best" assessment is the one that best serves the values at stake.

KINDS OF ASSESSMENT TASKS

Textbox 5.1 lists broad categories of assessments with examples in each category. It's not an exhaustive list or the only way to classify assessments.

TEXTBOX 5.1

ASSESSMENT TYPES

Test/Quiz: A set of questions a student must answer in order to demonstrate knowledge or skills in a particular area.

- Recitation
- Multiple choice
- Matching
- Problem-solving
- Short answer
- Constructed response (essay)

Composition: A piece of writing or other work that demonstrates understanding of a topic or theme under study. Students are sometimes asked to accompany nonverbal compositions (like graphs, collages, or models) with a written or spoken explanation.

- Review
- Research report
- Essay (comparison, analysis, interpretation)
- Lab report
- Advertisement
- Cartoon
- Graph
- Chart
- Diagram
- Map
- Drawing
- Collage
- Model

Case Study: A hypothetical or real-life incident allowing students to apply a range of skills and knowledge to a specific situation.

- Roleplay
- Mock Trial
- Skit
- Simulation

Oral Presentation: An opportunity for the student to speak about a particular topic or theme in order to convey his or her understanding of it. These might be considered to be spoken equivalents of responsive writing.

- Speech
- Retelling
- Poster session
- Multimedia presentation
- Documentary
- How-to video

(continued)

TEXTBOX 5.1. *(Continued)*

- Debate
- Socratic seminar
- Fishbowl discussion
- Panel discussion
- Interview

Performance: A complex, real-world task of the sort that practitioners in the field do.

- Lab
- Concert
- Game
- Art exhibition
- Dance
- Play
- Story
- Poem
- Graphic novel
- Op-ed
- Brochure
- Letter to an authority

Informal Self-Assessment: Ways for students to make their own learning visible, recognize areas of difficulty, and set new goals. These are often ongoing and happen concurrently with more formal, higher-stakes assessments.

- Journal
- Log
- Reflection
- Checklist
- Conference

Portfolio: A collection of work samples, displaying various skills and knowledge or indicating growth over time. Students compile these pieces of work and submit them together.

Student Choice Project: A project where students choose the form of their assessment (often from a "menu" or "choice board"). Ideally, all choices will measure the students' understanding of the same concepts or information.

Student work can serve multiple functions, and these functions can depend on the context in which the work is assigned. For example, a drawing in art class would be a performance assessment, where the student is doing what real-world artists do, while a drawing in science class would be a composition meant to communicate what the student has learned about bones. The point here isn't to get crazy about which category a particular assessment belongs to; it's to brainstorm possible assessments that will work with your curriculum.

Many assessment tasks also serve as instructional methods: Students learn concepts and skills in performing the task, and the end product is what the teacher looks at to see how much the student learned. The process of painting a portrait, playing a soccer game, doing a lab experiment, having a conversation in Chinese, or taking a multiple-choice history test helps students learn the skills to do these tasks so they'll be better at them the next time they do something similar.

The students will also learn content while performing assessment tasks; as they write an essay about the Vietnam War, they'll learn more about the Vietnam War, and as they take an algebra test, they're actually *learning* algebra as opposed to just demonstrating what they've learned already (Karpicke and Blunt 2011). An instructional task helps students learn; an assessment task shows the extent to which they learned—but students are always learning, even as they're being assessed. Maybe that's why teachers (and students) sometimes get confused between what counts as a learning activity and what counts as an assessment.

"VALUES-DENSE" ASSESSMENTS

"Nutrient density" refers to how much nutrition (protein, vitamins, minerals) is packed into the calories you ingest. Orange soda and orange juice have about the same number of calories per ounce, but the juice gives you vitamin C and potassium while the soda gives you nothing nutritionally useful.

Given that your time with your students is limited, it makes sense for each assessment task to be "values-dense," serving as many values as possible. Imagine that for her unit on *A Raisin in the Sun*, Allison stops assigning analytical essays about the play and instead has her students fictionalize an experience with injustice for the stage, much as the playwright Lorraine Hansberry did. While both tasks allow the students to learn transferable writing skills, the scene also lets the students use classic literature as a model for their own work and use their writing to take a stand against injustice—both of which are outcomes that Allison values. For her, the dramatic scene is a more "values-dense" assessment task.

The Assessment Swapping exercise in textbox 5.2 contains a series of prompts to help you clarify how well an assessment you're currently using (or thinking of using)

TEXTBOX 5.2

ASSESSMENT SWAPPING

1. Consider the assessment you're already using for your unit. Write or talk about how this assessment serves your values, using some or all of these questions:

   - How is this task a worthwhile use of my students' time?
   - How will this assessment help me see what my students have learned?
   - If my students can complete this assessment, what will they be able to do next?
   - Why did I choose to assess my students in this particular way?
   - Which of my values does this assessment serve?

2. From a list of assessment types, choose at least one that you might want to use for your unit but currently don't.

3. Write or talk about how the new assessment type(s) you identified might serve your values, using some or all of these questions:

   - How would this task be a worthwhile use of my students' time?
   - How could this assessment help me see what my students learned?
   - If my students could complete this assessment, what would they be able to do next?

- Why might I choose to assess my students in this particular way?

- Which of my values would this assessment serve?

4. Does it make sense to swap the assessment you currently use for one you don't—and still serve the same (or more) values? If it doesn't make sense to use this new assessment practice in your current unit, where else in your course might it go?

serves your values and decide if you want to swap out the assessment for another that even better serves your values.

If you find a more "values-dense" assessment type, you might wish to go through potential barriers to using it: beliefs about yourself that might stop you from giving this assessment, your unwillingness to experience any discomfort that giving this assessment might bring, and any external factors.

STUDENTS CHOOSING HOW THEY'RE ASSESSED

If several different assessments are equally values-dense, you might consider giving students a choice in how they're assessed. Choice is itself a value, and providing choices gives students a chance to serve their individual values—or at least their interests and strengths.

Imagine that a student who takes choral music with Nancy is talking to a friend who's in Hector's class. Nancy's student thinks it's embarrassing to solo in front of everyone and might be more likely to mess up as a result. Hector's student has trouble remembering which note goes with which letter but is perfectly capable of singing them all correctly. Now imagine that both chorus teachers realize that all they really want is to see how well their students understand musical notation, so they both decide to give their students a choice of how they want that knowledge assessed, through sight-singing or staff-labeling.

A danger in giving students choices in how they're assessed is that you might not be able to support them so they can all do well on all the different assessment options you're offering. If after reading *A Raisin in the Sun*, Allison's students chose between writing scenes dramatizing experiences with injustice and essays analyzing how the playwright portrayed injustices she encountered, she might not have time to provide the explicit teaching her students would need to ensure their success on both assignments.

Another problem with giving students choices is that different assessments might not be truly equal in how well they serve important values. If Hector wants his students keep records of their progress, he might be bothered that the sight-singing quiz provides no record. He could make audio files of their singing quizzes, but he might face logistical problems in getting the files to his students and making sure they listen to them. A folder full of graded quizzes is easy to flip through, so students can quickly see their progress and discover patterns in their mistakes. If these are key values, Hector probably won't use the sight-singing quiz.

If you're trying to decide whether to offer students a choice in how they're assessed, try making lists of values each assessment would serve, and see if the assessments are truly equal in their values density.

WHEN AND HOW OFTEN TO GIVE ASSESSMENTS

If a unit is a time-bound study of a particular topic, it often makes sense to assess the students' understanding of the topic at the end of that time period. What have they learned as a result of all the different experiences you've led them through?

If you value giving your students occasion to synthesize their understandings, then you might give one big assessment at the end of a unit. Many students feel stressed out by the prospect of one assessment measuring all the understandings amassed over several weeks or months, but the process of distilling mounds of notes into key understandings, and then applying those understandings to solve problems on a test or create something for a project, can be tremendously rewarding and exciting. Some students won't realize how much they've learned until they put the pieces together into a coherent whole.

Another option is to give mini-assessments throughout a unit. If you have the time and willingness to make and grade lots of little quizzes and projects, these can help you separate out discrete skills and subtopics, or they can reveal student progress over time. Giving more assessments allows you to act in accordance with more values: Why choose between the benefits of a lab report and a quiz when your students can have both? Since undoubtedly you'll have students whose own values are better served by one assessment than another, multiple assessments mean multiple opportunities to serve students' values, too.

HELPING STUDENTS REACH OUTCOMES YOU VALUE

Regardless of what kinds of assessments you give, if they are making visible the understandings that you value, then you probably want to ensure all your students are positioned to excel. Here are some ways to do that.

Provide Multiple Models of Excellent Work for Students to Analyze

Whether your students' task is to write papers on the Arab Spring or print properly formed lowercase letters, they need to see what the end products should look like.

Students who see only one model might not know which aspects are fundamental qualities of the product and which are idiosyncratic to that example.

Take a fifth grade teacher who wants his students to write about personal encounters with wildlife in the style of the articles he sometimes reads in nature magazines. He has trouble finding articles written at a fifth grade reading level that have the scientific and literary quality he wants his students to achieve, so he decides to write his own. It's about a time when he visited the Galapagos and watched two marine iguanas fight, and the conclusion has a line about how he wanted to help the iguanas make peace even though he knew it was silly to anthropomorphize animals.

Even though he has his students brainstorm lots of ways they could conclude their articles, about a third of the kids write that they anthropomorphized the animals they encountered and felt silly about it! If the students had opportunities to analyze multiple models, they would have discovered more ways nature writers can conclude their work and would have been better equipped to use their own creativity within the bounds of the assignment (and less likely to plagiarize their teacher's work).

Teach *All* the Skills Students Need to Do Well

A good assessment will require valued knowledge and skills that relate to your subject area, and it will probably also require skills that relate to the assessment task itself but not to your subject. Many kids are asked to make posters for school, but rarely are they taught the basics of effective poster design. Teachers might ask students to make videos without teaching them how to operate the camera, check the sound and lighting, or edit the footage. Some teachers mention task elements like these ("No white space on your posters!" or "Make sure I can hear you on the video!") but leave it to the students to figure out how to do them.

A good way to become aware of the full range of skills an assessment task requires is to do it yourself. Then, you can decide if you want to add lessons to your unit to teach the skills, modify the project so students don't need to use a skill you don't think is worth teaching in your class, or change the project entirely.

For example, a Spanish teacher who wants to assess her students' ability to use food words and command-form verbs is considering having her students film cooking demos of traditional foods from Spanish-speaking countries. As she thinks about the project, or does it herself, this teacher realizes that her students would have a lot of new skills to learn, like using a tripod or making a tasty empanada— and these aren't skills she (or her principal) values enough that she's willing to devote class time to teaching them. After all, her job is to make sure her students learn Spanish.

If the teacher wants to see how well her students can use food vocabulary and command-form verbs, she could have them demonstrate simpler food preparation tasks they already know how to do (like making a sandwich), do their demos in class instead of on video, or watch professional cooking shows on mute and narrate them in Spanish. In these ways, the teacher can keep the focus on assessing Spanish but still incorporate elements of her original idea.

As you decide whether to teach your students task-related skills outside your discipline, you might consider how your aesthetic values—as opposed to your teaching values—are impacting your assessment criteria. For a third grade unit on the rainforest, the teacher considers assessing her students' understanding of plant and animal adaptations and interactions by having them build a model rainforest theme park where each ride, game, or concession stand is based on an animal or plant. She pictures miniature spinning cup rides where the cups are pitcher plants, and roller coasters where the tracks are liana vines.

It all looks very cute in her mind, but her third graders wouldn't be able to create the models she's imagining, and she isn't about to take time away from reading or math to teach eight-year-olds how to make pitcher plants out of modeling clay. Anyway, she reasons, making a model rainforest theme park isn't going to assess the kids' understanding of rainforest plants and animals better than making and explaining drawings—so that's what her students do.

Allow Class Time for Students to Reach Your Expected Level of Quality

To complete products or prepare for performances (including performances on tests), students need time for individual or group work, peer and teacher conferencing and coaching, and ad-hoc mini-lessons. With all that can be happening during these work periods, classroom management becomes important—sometimes dauntingly so. Some teachers assign the product-making or performance-preparing as homework and hope their students will be able to meet expectations on their own. Often they won't. Again, if the assessment serves your values, then making sure students do well is probably worth the class time.

One way to help students make the most of a work period is to have them set goals for themselves. If they're old enough to write their goals on sticky notes, these notes will be easy for you to check quickly so you can support students who need to make their goals more specific, achievable, or appropriate to the assignment. For example, if a student says she wants to use a science work period to go over the math in her lab report, the teacher could ask what strategy she plans to use to check for errors (and teach her one if necessary). As the period continues, you can monitor students' progress on their goals and have them set new ones.

Another way to manage a class during a work period is to have each student sign up to do a particular type of work. For example, art students working on metalsmithing could have the options to attend a mini-lesson to review soldering, partner up for peer critiques, or work individually on cutting and hammering their pieces. Posting these sign-ups allows you to see at any moment whether your students are on or off task.

Modify Assignments to Fit Students' Needs

Just as real-world basketball teams play in tournaments, sixth graders could compete in their own tournament, with conditions of play modified to be appropriate for them. The sixth graders could play half-court games and get extra foul shots, and smaller classes could play in teams of three or four instead of the traditional five.

College basketball players' success is measured in points and wins, but a sixth grade P.E. student's success has more to do with developing new skills. Instead of focusing on which team wins or how many points each students get, the teachers could rate each student's competencies in dribbling, passing, shooting, and other basketball skills, as well as in fair play, leadership, and other relational skills associated with sports (and other domains of life).

WRITING ASSESSMENT GUIDELINES

Creating a values-dense assessment will mean writing—or rewriting—guidelines so your students know what you expect them to produce. You might give your students a list of things to do to complete the task well, or you might give them a description of a well-done product. If you describe the finished product in a rubric, you might provide performance scales for each criterion, such as "poor" to "excellent" or "emerging" to "expert," or you might simply list what you hope to see. However you write your criteria, it seems only fair that the students know what you'll be valuing when you examine their work.

Textbox 5.3 gives examples of values-congruent assessment guidelines, with intentional variety in how they look. These assessments come from units described in the last chapter (tables 4.2 and 4.3): a science unit on The Chesapeake Bay Watershed, a math unit on Graphing Functions in the Coordinate Plane, and an English unit called Poetry with Purpose.

Here are a few tips on writing assessment guidelines:

Consider What to Define and What to Leave Open-Ended

Students need parameters that are open-ended enough to provide room for them to take ownership of their work, yet defined enough to keep them from feeling overwhelmed by infinite possibilities or frustrated by the thought that there's some secret "right" way.

Imagine that in their physical science class, eighth graders build bridges using common household items to carry a load of at least thirty pounds but that can weigh no more than one hundred grams and be no longer than thirty centimeters. The students then test their bridges' strength, and the whole class makes a scatterplot graph of each bridge's efficiency ratio (the mass the bridge can hold relative to the mass of the bridge itself). On posters, the students display photos of real-world bridges of the same type as their model bridges, written discussions of their design processes, and graphs of class data.

This bridge project is defined enough that students understand the expectations, yet it leaves room for creative use of materials and design, and the implicit friendly competition over whose bridge will hold the most weight can be motivating. Which parameters you define and which you leave open depend on values.

TEXTBOX 5.3

VALUES-CONGRUENT ASSESSMENT GUIDELINES

Unit: The Chesapeake Bay Watershed
Assignment: "Using Water Quality Indicators" Lab Report

Give a clear, specific explanation of the purpose of testing water quality.	10	0	Give a vague or unclear explanation of the purpose of testing water quality.
Explain your hypothesis for how clean our water is, based on your knowledge from this course.	20	0	Write a hypothesis that doesn't fit what you've learned and/or is unclear.
Accurately list the materials you used to conduct the experiment.	10	0	Omit materials or describe them inaccurately.
Clearly describe the procedure you used.	10	0	Describe the procedure in a confusing way, so that a reader would need to ask lots of questions in order to understand what you did.
Organize observations and data in clear and accurate charts and tables.	20	0	Present observations and data in an unclear, disorganized, or inaccurate way.
Write a discussion in which you use data to support conclusions about the water quality.	30	0	Write conclusions about the water quality without referring to data to support it, or draw conclusions that are not supported by the data.

UNIT: GRAPHING FUNCTIONS IN THE COORDINATE PLANE
ASSIGNMENT: WHAT'S THE RELATIONSHIP?

Working in a group, you'll choose a question of interest to middle schoolers for which you can determine if there is a functional relationship, a correlation, or no relationship between two variables. For example, you might explore the relationship between hours of sleep and grades, money spent on clothes and self-esteem, or time spent with friends and happiness. You'll collect data, make a graph, present it to your classmates, and put the graph and a description of your findings on a mini-poster to put up in strategic places around the school to raise awareness about the issue.

Elements	Criteria	Score
RESEARCH QUESTION	You explored a question of interest to middle schoolers for which you can determine if there is a relationship between variables.	/10
DATA COLLECTION	You collected enough data to be able to see on a graph whether there is a relationship between your variables.	/15
DATA DISPLAY	Your scatterplot graph, best-fit line, and equation in slope-intercept form clearly and accurately showed the relationship between your variables.	/25
PRESENTATION	You were able to explain your graph to your classmates verbally and algebraically.	/25
	You spoke loudly and clearly enough during your presentation.	/5
MINI-POSTER	You used your classmates' comments and our class discussion to help you write a clear explanation of your findings and suggestions for behavior based on the data.	/15
	You put your graph and description into an eye-catching mini-poster.	/5

Comments:

UNIT: POETRY WITH PURPOSE

Assignment: Poetry Collection

Using the poems we read in class as models, create a collection of five original poems on one topic that matters to you.

I will look especially for these elements:

- Your precise vocabulary shows you've become an expert on your topic and are connected to it.

- Your concrete, specific imagery brings the subject fully to life.

- You effectively and purposefully used poetic devices such as repetition, onomatopoeia, assonance/consonance, juxtaposition, and metaphor.

(continued)

TEXTBOX 5.3. *(Continued)*

I will also look for these elements:

- Your words are original, with no clichés.
- The line and stanza breaks are meaningful.
- An introduction (at least one page) explains your connection to your topic, your development as a poet, and any messages you want to give your reader.
- Each poem has a meaningful title, and the collection itself has a meaningful title.
- The poems are easy to read because you proofread. There are no errors in capitalization, punctuation, or spelling to distract the reader. Grammatical departures are for stylistic purposes and are not merely incorrect.

Set Yourself Up to Give Values-Congruent Grades

For most assessments, you'll have several different expectations—and not all expectations will be equally valued. You can make sure your students know what you'll be looking at most when you're grading their work, both by telling them on the assignment guidelines and by devoting the most class time to the skills and understandings you'll be valuing on the assessment.

When Allison's students read *A Raisin in the Sun*, they look closely at how the playwright creates authentic characters with layered conflicts and distinct voices. When writing their own dramatic scenes, the students spend class time learning how to make characters seem authentic rather than stereotypical, create layered conflicts, and make each voice sound distinct. That's why when she's grading, Allison looks especially for her students' use of authentic characters, layered conflicts, and distinct voices. She looks for other things too, but what gets the most class time also gets the most weight in their grades.

Jason has a different system for giving values-congruent grades. He has his math students write explanations of where they went astray on problems they got wrong, and then they redo the problems correctly and get back at least some of their points. Jason values thoroughness and self-discipline in the problem-solving process, so he doesn't give partial credit. He values self-awareness, so his students analyze their errors, and resourcefulness, so they figure out for themselves how to get the correct solution. Finally, he values high achievement, so he doesn't let his students off the hook with only partially correct work.

Copy Valued Expectations from Assignment to Assignment

Every time Allison's seventh graders write an essay, she teaches them how to use specific evidence to support their points. By the end of the year, the kids can recite her expectation verbatim because it's on every essay assignment sheet, and they know it's an important aspect of writing a strong essay.

Since each assignment is different, Allison tells her students what their evidence should consist of in each essay. Her assignment sheet for essays about neighborhood success stories includes this guideline: "You support your thesis with specific evidence. In this case, your evidence should include images and stories of someone or something successful in your neighborhood." Later in the year, when her students write essays about activists whose memoirs they read, the assignment sheet includes this: "You support your thesis with specific evidence. In this case, your evidence should include images and stories of your activist."

Look for the Impact of Unintended Bias

Many teachers value accuracy, but giving points for correct spelling and grammar might mean kids whose parents or guardians speak English and are home to provide homework help (or can pay tutors) end up with better grades. Some teachers value participation in class, but if participation is only defined as "raising your hand and talking a lot," then kids with particular ethnic backgrounds and gender-conforming behaviors might be privileged.

If you discover unfair outcomes, you can look for alternative ways to avoid them and still serve your values. For example, participation in a class can mean contributing to a large- or small-group discussion, and it can mean speaking, writing, and active listening.

PROJECT-BASED ASSESSMENTS AND VALUES

Many of the assessments described in this chapter are "projects." Usually, the valued goal of a unit is not just for students to remember information but also to understand and apply important concepts. For example, in a unit on cell structures, students would not just be able to recite the names and functions of organelles; they'd also reach a deeper understanding of how organelles work together for different purposes, how their structures relate to their functions, and how different types of cells have different shapes and parts to fulfill different functions for the organism.

What you value in a unit—what matters about the topic or skill under study—often involves your students applying skills they're learning in new contexts, analyzing and evaluating situations, and create new things and ideas. These are all forms of higher-order thinking. The revised Bloom's Taxonomy (Krathwohl 2002) distinguishes six levels of cognitive processing: (1) retrieving knowledge, (2) determining meaning (i.e., "reading" texts or images), (3) applying understandings to new situations, (4) analyzing how the parts of a thing relate to each other and to the whole, (5) making judgments based on evaluative criteria, and (6) creating original products.

Often it's easier to assess student learning lower down on Bloom's scale. For example, an assessment for a unit on cells could consist of students labeling a cell diagram's organelles and writing their functions; such a test would be easy to write and grade, but all the students would be doing is retrieving knowledge of organelle names and functions. If the reason you value getting your students to know or be able to do something is that you want them to apply and analyze it, or to use it to judge or create things, then it makes sense for your assessment tasks to demand these higher-level processes.

It's certainly possible to write test questions that require students to apply, analyze, judge, and create. For example, a teacher giving a test on landforms could have his students label a United States map using terms like "peninsula" and "bay," draw their own maps that include these features, or write about what life is like in these kinds of places. However, using higher-level thinking processes usually entails making plans, testing thinking, sharing, getting feedback, and tinkering with the work. And usually, when you've designed a task that allows students to do all that, it's a project.

Put much more simply, in a values-congruent unit, you want students to do important stuff with what they learn in your class. If you want to see if the students can do important stuff, then you need to give them important stuff to do! That "important stuff to do" is often a project.

ADJUSTING SOME MORE

On the day you begin a new unit, you can let your students know what the major assignment will be. That way, as they work through the unit, they know what they'll eventually be asked to do. By the time you give out the list of guidelines, your students will have already started the process of working on the assignment. Some teachers even give out the guidelines on the first day of the unit, but you might come up with better ideas for the assessment during class discussions.

Your purpose, finding out how much your students understand, can always be accomplished through many different tasks. If as you're teaching your unit, you come up with a new assessment idea, ask yourself if it better serves your values.

6

Aligning a Unit

How can you make sure the parts of your unit work together?

Can you think of an example of alignment, where the parts of something must fit together in a particular way for it to fulfill its purpose?

The wheels of a car must all be positioned at the correct angles in order for the car to go straight instead of veering off. A juicy burger, crispy fries, and some cold beer complement each other's tastes and textures for a perfectly aligned (if not that healthy) meal. In a curriculum, too, it makes a difference when the parts—essential questions, lessons, and assessments—are aligned.

Neurologist-turned-teacher Judy Willis ("A Neurologist" 2011) explains the brain chemistry behind why students learn better when they can connect daily lessons to an achievable and important end goal. When they feel they're making progress toward a valued outcome, a rush of dopamine "rewards" their brains in two ways: it makes them feel pleasure, which is motivating, and it reinforces the neural pathway they used to achieve the progress, which helps them repeat the behaviors that got them to that progress.

Willis describes how in video games, each task has a clear objective (get past this baddie), and the ultimate goal of the game is also clear (save the city). Increasing scores, levels, and powers provide tangible evidence of accomplishment as well as motivation to keep going toward the final goal. Curriculum is no different: The students need to see an ultimate goal, a clear purpose to each learning task, and how each task represents progress toward the goal.

Willis also explains that students better retain ideas and skills, and transfer them to new situations, when these ideas and skills make sense in an overall context: "Information learned by rote memorization will not enter the sturdy long-term neural networks in the prefrontal cortex unless students have the opportunity to actively recognize relationships to their prior knowledge and/or apply new learning to new situations" ("Three Brain-Based Teaching Strategies" 2011).

In order for students to feel motivated to learn, and to learn in a way that will stick, the lessons within a unit must work toward a valued purpose as articulated in essential questions, make sense in the context of the unit, and result in a well-defined end product, the assessment task. The parts of the unit need to be aligned.

A VALUES-ALIGNED UNIT

What does an aligned unit look like? When Laurie was bringing Sherman Alexie's novel *The Absolutely True Diary of a Part-Time Indian* into her English 6 curriculum, she thought a lot about why. It brought in a Native American voice, but there were other books by Native American authors and other groups of voices the program lacked. *Part-Time Indian* is an award-winning book by a famous and respected author, but again, there are lots of award-winning books by famous and respected authors. What about this particular book mattered? What did Laurie most want her students to get out of reading it?

The Absolutely True Diary of a Part-Time Indian tells the story of Arnold, a boy who is growing up on the Spokane Indian reservation in Washington state. Arnold's academic and artistic capabilities aren't nurtured at the "rez" school, so he decides to attend Reardan, an all-white school twenty-two miles away. The book is about Arnold's struggle to code-switch between his two worlds, trying to define his identity as a member of Reardan and the reservation instead of feeling like he belonged to neither. The story is also hysterically funny.

Laurie saw three elements as important. First, as a story about identities in conflict, *Part-Time Indian* could give the sixth graders insights into their own identity conflicts and into lives beyond their own. Second, the book tells a personal story through words and pictures, and as a storyteller herself, Laurie valued giving her students access to different ways people tell their stories. Finally, Laurie wants her students to use the literary devices they encounter in texts, and Sherman Alexie is a master of creating humor by exaggerating events.

Laurie realized that the very title of the book reflected the three things she'd identified as important: the story was "Absolutely True" in that it used hyperbole to emphasize key events in funny ways, it was a "Diary" that used multiple media to tell a personal story, and it was about a "Part-Time Indian" whose identities were in conflict with each other and with his communities.

Once she had thought through her values in teaching this book, Laurie was able to write the essential questions *What happens when different parts of our identity are in conflict?* and *What does it mean for a story to be "true"?* These essential questions became the basis of all of her lessons during that unit:

- Finding passages where Arnold "introduces himself" to the reader, to get at his various identities.
- Analyzing ways Arnold's identities were in conflict with each other and with his environments. These discussions included the concept of code-switching, or changing the ways we express ourselves based on the cultural codes of our surroundings.
- Brainstorming lots of ways the students defined their own identities.
- Telling stories about particular times in the students' lives when an identity conflict surfaced.
- Discussing purposes of hyperbole, identifying examples of hyperbole in the book, and using hyperbole in their personal stories.

The unit's assessment task reflected all that the students had learned and also aligned with the essential question: "Using *The Absolutely True Diary of a Part-Time Indian* as a model, write an 'absolutely true' short story based on a specific incident from your life in which you experienced a conflict related to your identity. This could be a time when two of your identities were in conflict with each other or a time when an identity of yours was in conflict with the world around you."

In Laurie's well-aligned unit, every lesson moves the students toward an understanding of the key concepts. Those understandings become visible on the assessment. Laurie teaches the skills and knowledge she expects her students to use in order to do well on the assessment, and her students constantly and recursively explore key ideas. Each lesson builds meaningfully on the last, so that when students come into the room, they already can guess what they'll be doing that day, and when they're about to leave, they know what the homework will be even before it's announced.

Laurie's unit isn't the only or "right" way to approach the book (though the way it reflects the title is rather elegant). The conceptual focus for a unit about this book could just as easily be coming of age, semi-autobiographical fiction, or stereotypes. The "right" unit depends on the individual teacher's and the school's values. The point here is that aligning the lessons, assessment, and essential question will help students fit new knowledge into an overall framework of meaning and to understand what's expected of them—which helps them learn in a deeper and more lasting way.

RESISTANCE TO ALIGNMENT

Some teachers argue that a carefully aligned curriculum feels too prescribed and leaves no room for students to come up with their own creative ideas, or for the teachers to respond to students' questions or to local and world events that feel immediate and weighty. What if a topic comes up but has nothing to do with your essential question? What if a student thinks up a different idea you hadn't expected?

Students can and will make accidental discoveries and creative connections. You can design opportunities within your curriculum for students to do these things. And if you're moved to bring in a topic or lesson that doesn't connect to the unit but seems important, then do it! Stand-alone lessons can be opportunities to bring in more of what you and your students value. As long as you explain what you're doing, your students won't lose the bigger picture of the unit. A willingness to leave room for student creativity and to be responsive doesn't mean you can't *also* plan experiences that will lead students to valued understandings.

A second argument against aligned curriculum is that its predictability would make it boring for students. For sure, novelty is exciting and can engender curiosity, which motivates students to learn. In an aligned unit, novelty can come in the form of new topics or new angles on old ones, unexpected lesson formats, and projects that require discovery. At the same time, students feel motivated to pay attention when a lesson feels meaningful—when it fits into a larger picture.

Donella Meadows and Diana Wright (2008) define a system as "an interconnected set of elements that is coherently organized in a way that achieves something" (11). An aligned unit works as a system: It features interconnected essential questions, content, skills, and assessments that are coherently organized into lessons that work together to achieve something we value.

GETTING ALIGNED

A good essential question is like the picture on the puzzle box: It helpfully shows you an image to strive for, but it's still up to you to put all the pieces together to create that image. And designing a curriculum isn't actually like putting together a jigsaw puzzle, where every piece will snap into a specific place. It's more like creating a tile mosaic, where there are all kinds of ways you can create the picture in your sketch, and sometimes you have to reshape the pieces so they fit together.

If you're trying to achieve alignment among your unit's essential question, lessons, and assessment, figure 6.1 has a template that might help you.

The arrows in the template indicate two possible paths outward from an essential question. One path, which follows the arrows in an "L" shape, begins with designing an assessment that will show you that the students truly got the valued concepts. Once you've decided what excellence would look like on that assessment, the content and skills your students need in order to achieve that excellence become the topics of your lessons. In a way, this path is "teaching to the test," if "test" means a traditional test, essay, painting, or anything that lets you see how well your students understand the content and can perform the skills you value.

It certainly makes sense to think first about how you'll know the students got the concept and then decide on the best lessons that will lead students to be successful on the assessment; that's backward design. It's also not how many teachers tend to think.

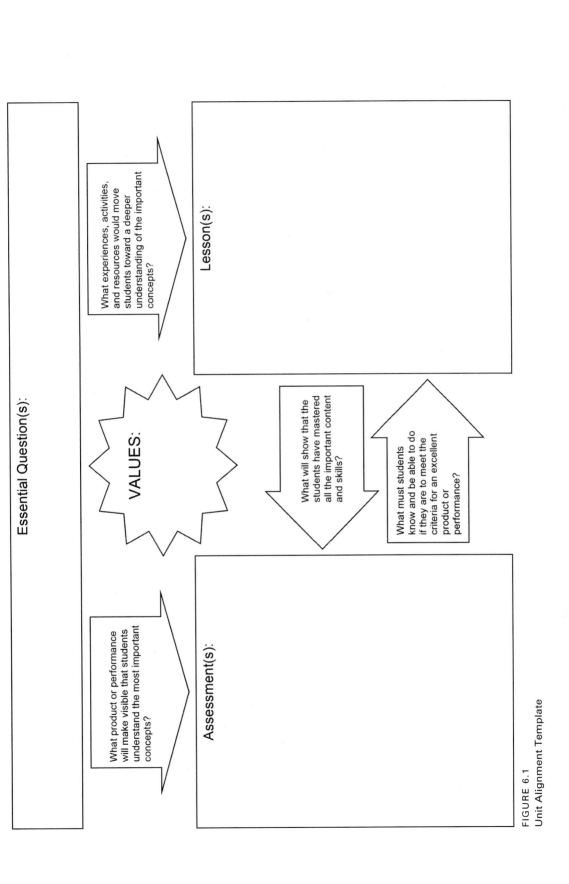

Essential Question(s):

What experiences, activities, and resources would move students toward a deeper understanding of the important concepts?

Lesson(s):

VALUES:

What will show that the students have mastered all the important content and skills?

What must students know and be able to do if they are to meet the criteria for an excellent product or performance?

What product or performance will make visible that students understand the most important concepts?

Assessment(s):

FIGURE 6.1
Unit Alignment Template

In another path, the "d," you still start with an essential question, and then you ask yourself what lessons you'll need to teach and in what order so your students reach a deep understanding of the valued concept. Next, you figure out an assessment that will make that understanding visible. Then, you double back (completing the "d" shape) to make sure you've incorporated lessons where you're actually teaching students the knowledge and skills you expect them to use on a well-done assessment.

Neither the "d" nor the "L" is inherently better; the path that works better for you will be the one that leads you to design units that match your values. That's why, "d" or "L," you can finish the unit design process by looking over the whole plan to see if everything matches your values and any other values that impact your curriculum—such as those your department and school hold, and those embedded in standards.

Figures 6.2, 6.3, and 6.4 show examples of what the unit alignment template looks like when it's filled out. You might recognize the high school fitness, eighth-grade English, and fifth-grade social studies units from chapter 2.

COMMON PROBLEMS IN ALIGNING A UNIT

Even teachers who solidly understand how to write essential questions, lessons, and assessments still have all kinds of difficulties aligning them. These case studies show common problems that surface when a unit's parts aren't aligned. As you read them, try coming up with your own ideas for what these teachers could do to align their units. You might even read these case studies with a colleague or two, and if some of the problems sound familiar, try helping each other address them.

Problem: When the Lessons and Assessment Don't Match the Essential Question

Wendy wrote this essential question for her sixth-grade American history class: *How could there be slavery in a nation founded on equality?* Students learned about the daily lives of enslaved African Americans, including what they did to build U.S. infrastructures and the ways they resisted slavery. For an assessment, groups of students created children's museum exhibits that taught about African American culture, work, and resistance during slavery. Wendy was pleased with the depth of thought her students put into their work and by how strong their understandings were.

Wendy's question asks about how the United States justified the existence of slavery, but her unit is about the lives of people who were enslaved. Her essential question isn't a bad one; it just has nothing to do with her unit—other than that they're both on the broad topic of slavery in the United States.

This kind of mismatch between a unit and its essential question is surprisingly common. Some teachers might figure out how to write meaty-sounding questions without clarifying their values for the unit, and they end up teaching what they value and ignoring the question. If that's true for Wendy, she simply needs to change her essential question to reflect the unit she actually teaches—something like *What was life like for*

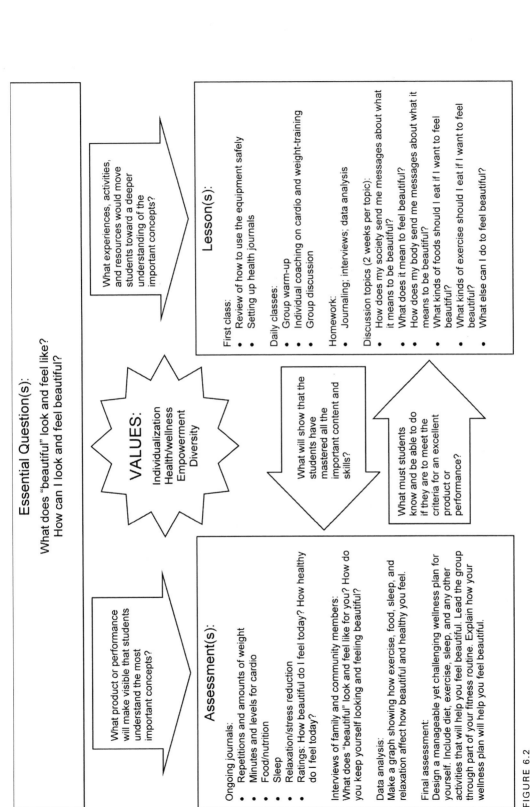

Essential Question(s):

What does "beautiful" look and feel like?
How can I look and feel beautiful?

What product or performance will make visible that students understand the most important concepts?

What experiences, activities, and resources would move students toward a deeper understanding of the important concepts?

VALUES:
Individualization
Health/wellness
Empowerment
Diversity

What will show that the students have mastered all the important content and skills?

What must students know and be able to do if they are to meet the criteria for an excellent product or performance?

Lesson(s):

First class:
- Review of how to use the equipment safely
- Setting up health journals

Daily classes:
- Group warm-up
- Individual coaching on cardio and weight-training
- Group discussion

Homework:
- Journaling; interviews; data analysis

Discussion topics (2 weeks per topic):
- How does my society send me messages about what it means to be beautiful?
- What does it mean to feel beautiful?
- How does my body send me messages about what it means to be beautiful?
- What kinds of foods should I eat if I want to feel beautiful?
- What kinds of exercise should I eat if I want to feel beautiful?
- What else can I do to feel beautiful?

Assessment(s):

Ongoing journals:
- Repetitions and amounts of weight
- Minutes and levels for cardio
- Food/nutrition
- Sleep
- Relaxation/stress reduction
- Ratings: How beautiful do I feel today? How healthy do I feel today?

Interviews of family and community members:
What does "beautiful" look and feel like for you? How do you keep yourself looking and feeling beautiful?

Data analysis:
Make a graph showing how exercise, food, sleep, and relaxation affect how beautiful and healthy you feel.

Final assessment:
Design a manageable yet challenging wellness plan for yourself. Include diet, exercise, sleep, and any other activities that will help you feel beautiful. Lead the group through part of your fitness routine. Explain how your wellness plan will help you feel beautiful.

FIGURE 6.2
An Aligned Unit (High School Fitness)

Essential Question(s):

How do books both perpetuate and challenge stereotypes?

What experiences, activities, and resources would move students toward a deeper understanding of the important concepts?

Lesson(s):

Week 1 (reading Book 1):
- Identify stereotypes related to gender, class, and religion.
- How does the text perpetuate and challenge stereotypes?

Week 2 (reading Book 2):
- Do critical readings deconstructing the stereotypes in *Bread Givers.*
- Book round robin activity: How do books appeal to male and female readers? How does this relate to stereotypes?

Week 3 (finishing the book and starting the trial):
- Explain trial format and assign roles.
- Work in groups to look for evidence of how the book perpetuates and challenges stereotypes.

Week 4 (writing essays):
- Finish the trial.
- Write an essay analyzing how a particular stereotype works in the text.

VALUES:

Reading closely and critically
Positioning all to succeed

What will show that the students have mastered all the important content and skills?

What must students know and be able to do if they are to meet the criteria for an excellent product or performance?

What product or performance will make visible that students understand the most important concepts?

Assessment(s):

1. Put *Bread Givers* on trial for perpetuating stereotypes about gender, class, and religion. Each member of the class will serve as a plaintiff's attorney, who will argue that the book perpetuates stereotypes, or a defense attorney, who will argue that the book challenges stereotypes.

2. Write an essay in which you analyze how a particular stereotype works in *Bread Givers.* Support your thesis with specific quotations from the text.

FIGURE 6.3

Aln Aigned Unit (Eighth Grade English)

Essential Question(s):

How do groups of people use, abuse, and protect their environments?

What experiences, activities, and resources would move students toward a deeper understanding of the important concepts?

Lesson(s):

Weeks 1-3: Our natural environment
- Neighborhood walk
- Online map exploration
- United States map collage using recycled materials

Weeks 4-5: How we use, abuse, and protect our natural environment
- Family interviews and share-out
- Readings

Weeks 6-8: How pre-contact Native American groups used, abused, and protected their natural environments
- Group research: homes, foods, clothing, art, and methods of subsistence
- Art-based presentations

Weeks 9-10: How Native American activist groups are building coalitions to fight for environmental protection
- Virtual visits from members of Native American activist groups
- Journaling

Weeks 11-12: How we can protect our environment
- Family interviews and share-out
- Action plans

VALUES:

Engagement
Critical Inquiry
Relevance
Sustainability

What will show that the students have mastered all the important content and skills?

What must students know and be able to do if they are to meet the criteria for an excellent product or performance?

What product or performance will make visible that students understand the most important concepts?

Assessment(s):

1. Use recycled materials to collage a physical map of the United States.

2. Critical thinking questions after family interview share-outs and readings: How do we use, abuse, and protect our natural environment?

3. Use the art form of your choice to show how pre-contact Native American groups used, abused, and protected their environments. You will work in a group. Each group will choose one of these topics: homes, foods, clothing, art, or a different topic your group proposes.

4. Write an essay that explains different ways various groups protect the environment.

5. Use everything you've learned about your natural environment and the ways people use, abuse, and protect their environments to write an action plan for how you will protect our environment.

FIGURE 6.4
An Aligned Unit (Fifth Grade Social Studies)

enslaved African Americans? or *How did enslaved African Americans resist the conditions of their enslavement?* If you end up with an essential question that doesn't match your unit, one option is to write a new question that does.

Another option is to write new lessons and assessments that fit the essential question you already have. Some units don't match their essential questions because the teacher doesn't know how to teach the content that *would* match the question and reverts to teaching content that's familiar and comfortable. If that's Wendy's problem, she'd probably need to increase her own knowledge about justifications for the existence of slavery in the United States. She might also need to ask for support in designing new lessons and writing a new assessment.

It's also possible to make the unit longer and have lessons and assessments about both essential questions. Wendy could keep her old unit, but use a more fitting essential question, *and* add lessons about how slavery was justified—but that would mean adding time to the unit or cutting some content.

Problem: When the Teacher Values Knowledge or Skills but Doesn't Explicitly Teach Them

Quentin was excited to add Marjane Satrapi's memoir *Persepolis* into his ninth-grade English curriculum. His essential question was, *How reliable is a child narrator?* His students examined ways the author made Marji an unreliable narrator, and Quentin assessed his students by having them write essays analyzing Marji's reliability. The essays were all pretty similar, and Quentin wanted to give his students more of an opportunity to put themselves into their writing. He also wanted to take better advantage of the fact that *Persepolis* is a graphic novel.

The next year, he added the question, *How do graphic novels dramatize conflict?* For the assessment, he gave this task: "Create a graphic story dramatizing a moment in your childhood that you didn't fully understand at the time." He was excited to read the graphic stories, but when he did, he was dismayed. The students hadn't understood how to use graphic storytelling techniques like panels and gutters, or how speech bubbles, thought bubbles, and narration served different functions—even though he'd told them! Worse, many students had picked moments in their childhoods that didn't seem all that important.

Quentin seems to value his students writing about what authentically matters to them and learning to use in their own writing the devices they encounter in their reading. When his students' essays all sounded the same, he changed the assignment to one that he thought would invite students to put more of themselves into their work. The problem was that he didn't *teach* them how to find genuinely important moments from their childhoods. Just because he gave the kids space to do something he thought they'd enjoy didn't mean they'd automatically do it. Also, though he pointed out some of the features of graphic novels, he didn't *teach* them in such a way that his students learned them.

Disappointment in your students' work can indicate that you're not teaching them the knowledge and skills you value. If you find that lots of your students are turning in work that disappoints you, try identifying the criteria for what you'd consider an excellent piece of work, and then include lessons in the unit where you teach the skills and knowledge students will need to fulfill those criteria. You might also do the assignment yourself and notice the skills and knowledge you need to use so you can later teach them to your students.

Since Quentin thinks a successful story sounds like it was important in the student's life, he could add a lesson where his students identify what's important to the author of *Persepolis* and then find moments in their childhoods that reflect what's important to them. He could also have his students analyze how different textual features of graphic novels serve different functions and plan out how they'll use these features to tell their own stories.

Problem: When the Assessment Task Measures What's Easy to Measure Instead of Valued Understandings

Mila, a seventh-grade math teacher, uses the essential question *How can I use unit rates to help me make decisions?* for her unit on ratios, rates, and proportions. After teaching her students how to calculate unit rates, she poses the following problem: "I am trying to decide among three different cars to buy. I live in Manhattan and drive to the Bronx every weekday, and I like to take long road trips during my summers. Local gas prices are going up, and we might experience gas shortages. Which car would be the most cost-effective option for me?"

She shows her students how to research car prices and miles per gallon rates, map her yearly highway and city mileage, and set up algebraic equations to calculate her approximate yearly gas expenditures in order to figure out which car she should buy. On their unit test, the students successfully use cross products to solve proportions, convert between fractions or decimals and percentages, and use equations to solve word problems. A few days after the unit ends, Mila's principal notices the essential question still posted on her wall. He asks a student, "So, how *can* you use unit rates to help you make decisions?" The student, who's getting an A in math, can't answer.

Mila seems to value teaching her students how they can use algebra in real life, and her essential question, *How can I use unit rates to help me make decisions?*, reflects that value. Her problem is that the test tells her only how well her students are able to solve algebra problems, and they were able to do perfectly well on that test without demonstrating any understanding of the bigger idea of how to use unit rates to help them make decisions.

If your assessment task measures what's easy to measure instead of valued understandings, you won't know if your students got the bigger idea, and your students might think the easy-to-measure stuff was the point. If you find that you can't tell from the assessment whether students got the bigger idea, you can either change the assessment task so it makes valued understandings visible or create a series of assessment tasks that measure different understandings.

Next year, Mila might try creating a project where the students use the math to help them make decisions in their own lives. Choosing a car might be relevant for Mila herself, but it isn't a decision her thirteen-year-old students are making. Mila could give them another problem like the car problem to work on independently or in groups. Or, she could guide her students through a brainstorm of ways they could use unit rates to help them make decisions, like which phone plan would be most cost-effective or which kinds of snacks would fit their levels of activity during the day.

The students could give oral or written reports on how they used rates, proportions, and percentages to help them make their decisions and how they could use similar math to help them make other kinds of decisions as they get older. If, after all of that, Mila feels she needs to assess her students' use of the algebra further, she can certainly give the test too.

Problem: When Teachers Assume Students Will Construct Valued Understandings for Themselves

Carlos loves to use a wide variety of teaching strategies to reach his eighth-grade science students. For his current unit on genetics, his essential question is *Should we change our genetic traits just because we can?* His students are extracting DNA from bananas, watching a film about genetically modified crops, acting out DNA replication, reading a science fiction story about the ethics of genetic manipulation in humans, playing a game to learn how genes mutate, and reading articles about new gene therapies.

For their assessment, the students are having a series of debates over whether we should modify the genetic traits of various organisms. As his students are preparing their arguments, Carlos is getting very frustrated. He keeps having to tell them how the material they've seen in class supports or refutes their arguments. "We learned this," he keeps saying. "Think—the answer is right in front of you!"

Carlos's situation is a great example of how an essential question like *Should we change our genetic traits just because we can?* isn't an automatic safeguard against ringmaster-style teaching—that is, guiding students through a series of exciting activities without a clear point or purpose to it all. Carlos's students might be fully engaged in each activity, but his deeper value seems to be getting them to connect their understandings of science to social and ethical issues. He needs to turn his series of lessons into a more meaningful progression of ideas.

If you find that your students aren't reaching the understandings you value, one solution is to resequence your lessons. In organizing his unit, Carlos could begin with the basics (DNA structure, replication, and mutation) and then move into lessons on genetic manipulation. He might even break the unit into two parts with separate essential questions and assessments for each part. The foundational lessons could comprise one unit, with a question like *How does DNA work?*, and a test or project could show if his students are solid on the basic concepts before moving into a unit on the biology and ethics of genetic manipulation.

Another way to help make sure students are connecting each lesson to the essential question is to make those connections clear and explicit. As his students move through the DNA unit, Carlos should continually revisit the question, *Should we change our genetic traits just because we can?*, perhaps by posting it and getting his students to discuss how each lesson informs their thinking about it. That way, they'll be more prepared to debate specific instances of genetic manipulation on their own.

Problem: When the Essential Question Seems So Important That the Unit Goes on Too Long

Tali teaches high school French II. Midway through the year, she teaches vocabulary associated with daily schedules, as well as reflexive verb conjugations, so students can say things like "I brush my teeth every morning" and "History class is second period." Tali wants her students to appreciate differences between their daily schedules and those of students in French-speaking countries, so she redesigns her unit using the essential question, *How does where I live influence my daily schedule?*

Her students read stories set in various Francophone countries, write a series of compositions describing daily life in different places, and look at websites from high schools in France, Quebec, Senegal, and Haiti to note similarities and differences between those school schedules and their own. Tali even arranges a video call with a class in Brussels so the students can interview each other about life in each place. Tali's students then give oral presentations on how daily schedules are similar and different for high school students in different places, and they take a test on the vocabulary and grammar they've learned.

The students work on this unit for more than a month and start asking when they're going to learn something new. At the end of the year, Tali runs out of time and can't teach the clothing unit. Her students are upset that they don't get to do the fashion show project they've seen older students do and will have to complete a grammar packet over the summer in order to be ready for French III in the fall.

Tali is very clear on her values: She wants her students to appreciate cultural similarities and differences, and to use French grammar and vocabulary in their speaking and writing. Her essential question, content, skills, and assessment are all perfectly aligned, but the unit goes on for so long that it takes time away from another valued unit, and the students get frustrated.

A unit that matches your values is a good problem to have! To avoid spending too much time on that unit—to the point that your students lose interest or you run out of time for other units—you can plan out how many lessons it will take to address each essential question and to teach the content and skills your students need for the assessment. If the unit seems like it will take too long, see if you can eliminate some content, teach some of the skills in a different unit, or modify the assessment so you stay within the time frame you've allotted.

Tali should decide how long to make the unit, given what her students need to gain from it but also in context of her other units. Using that time frame, she can choose which content, skills, and assessments are most important and design effective but less time-consuming learning activities. Perhaps each student could choose a country, read one story set there, and write a composition to read to the class. Or they could all read two stories and write compositions that compare and contrast daily life in the two places. Tali could eliminate the test and use the composition and presentation to assess vocabulary and grammar mastery.

Tali could even write an essential question for the clothing unit that parallels her essential question for the daily life unit, moving her students from *How does where I live influence my daily schedule?* to *How does where I live influence my clothing choices?* Her students could do similar work for the two units, thus deepening their understandings of cultural similarities and differences, learning even more French grammar and vocabulary, and doing even more French speaking and writing.

ASSESSING YOUR UNIT

If aligning a unit is such a challenge, how do you know if you've done it? And if you have an alignment problem, what can you do about it? Textbox 6.1 is a self-assessment tool you can use after teaching a unit to help you think about how to revise it for

---

TEXTBOX 6.1

SELF-ASSESSMENT FOR VALUES ALIGNMENT

Does the student work match my values?

- What further criteria do I need to articulate?
- What lessons do I need to add so students have the knowledge and skills to do better work?
- Do I need to change the assessment task entirely?

Do the essential questions match what I ended up teaching and assessing?

- How can I change the question to make it accurately reflect what I taught?
- Should I add another essential question?

Can I tell from the assessment task that the students got the bigger idea?

- How can I change the assessment task so it measures their understanding?
- How I create a series of assessment tasks that measure different aspects of their understanding?

Were the lessons sequenced in a way that helped my students understand important concepts?

- How should I change the order?

Did I explain how each lesson connects to the essential questions? To my values?

- How can I build in opportunities to make the purpose clearer to my students?
- How can I explain how each lesson fits into the bigger conceptual picture of the unit?

Did this unit take an acceptable length of time?

- What content can I eliminate?
- What skills can I move into a different unit?
- How can I simplify the assessment? Are there criteria I can eliminate?

the following year. The questions are designed to help you decide what to keep, cut, change, or rearrange.

Your best indicator of whether your unit matches your values will usually be the students' work. If something about their work disappoints you or seems "off," that's a sign that you might need to redesign the assessment, add a lesson, or even change the essential question.

Another great way to check your unit's alignment is to talk through it and see where you get stuck, begin to feel uncomfortable, or find yourself rationalizing your choices. These might be places where you're encountering barriers to values-congruent action that could result in alignment difficulties. If you're talking to a colleague, he or she might notice alignment problems too and give suggestions for how you can overcome them.

7

Designing a Values-Congruent Course

How can you design an entire course around what matters most?

In nature, you'll find wholes within wholes—systems within systems, like cells making up organs making up organisms making up ecosystems. You'll also see systems within systems in the human-made world: households within neighborhoods within cities, or classrooms within schools within districts. A curriculum, too, is made up of wholes within wholes. Lessons make up units, which make up courses, which make up academic programs.

The way you design a unit will depend not only on the valued goals for that unit, but also on the course, program, school, and community in which your unit is situated. Though you might not have the decision-making power to make all the changes you want to make, you can start conversations with your colleagues and administrators about designing values-congruent courses and programs. Also—to borrow a phrase from the environmental movement—you can think "globally" (in terms of your course, program, and school) and act "locally" by working on your units.

COURSES AS HEAPS

Even if each unit has the integrity of a system, an overall course can still feel like a heap. One way to tell if your course is a heap is to try giving it a name. Can you call it something like American History or Life Science, which already sounds pretty broad in scope, or do you have to go even broader and call it something like English 7? Other than the fact that it's for seventh graders and that it's "English," the course might not be coherently organized in a way that will ensure it achieves something. It isn't a system; it's a heap.

Many courses are heaps of related content, like American History and Life Science. The Common Core standards, in contrast, relate mostly to skills so that students graduating from American high schools "are prepared to enter credit-bearing entry courses in two- or four-year college programs or enter the workforce" (NGA Center for Best Practices and CCSSO 2012) with the ability to do things that will help them succeed.

While the Common Core's emphasis on skills is a helpful reminder that students should learn how to *do* things rather than just absorb knowledge, adding a skills scope and sequence on top of the existing content scope and sequence doesn't do much to organize the curriculum into a system. If anything, the curriculum becomes more of a heap: Now you have to cover the mass of content in the textbook *and* the skills in the Core.

Schools often face pressure to keep adding more to the heap. More writing, more reading, more technology. More play time but also more work time. More music and art and test prep. How to make time for it all? More hours in the school day? More days in the academic year? More homework? And how do we make sure we're achieving "more?" More tests! No wonder teachers and students end up exhausted by June.

With all that schools try to incorporate, courses can easily become heaps of topics, processes, and materials. But if your students are to feel an ongoing sense of purpose and to learn in a way that is more likely to transfer to the next unit (or the next year), your entire course must be a meaningful, integrated whole. A system. Values can help you make more intentional decisions about how to organize your course so it works as a meaningful system.

ONGOING STRANDS

As you're thinking about how to organize your course, it's worth noticing that there's more to it than the sum of its units. Consider a science teacher who incorporates the theme of diversity into every unit, or a French teacher who gives weekly conversational skills checks regardless of what her students are learning, or an English teacher who has her students examine how each author they study uses a particular part of speech or sentence construction that they then use in whatever they're writing for that unit.

Elements of a course that recur throughout the year rather than being tied to specific units are called strands. If a unit is one dish and the course is the whole meal, a strand is like the beverage—an integral aspect of the meal that isn't part of any one dish. Strands can be recurring practices, such as using grammar in context, checking work for errors, staying safe in a lab, or warming up before game play. Strands can be recurring themes, such as sustainability, discrimination, change, or fairness. They can also be ongoing assessments that don't relate to any one unit, like a daily warm-up, a weekly skill check, or a project students are working on all year.

Strands can help give a sense of wholeness to your course and are another way to teach by your values. Essential questions can direct attention to what's important about your strands, get students interested in them, and help you decide what should and shouldn't be part of the strand. If you want to write essential questions for your course's strands, try using one of the "Finding What's Essential" protocols (textbox 3.1 or 3.2), using your strand as the area of focus.

COURSE-LEVEL ESSENTIAL QUESTIONS

Just as you can write essential questions for units and strands, you can write them for your entire course. Course-level questions direct attention to what's most important in the course, pique the students' curiosity about the subject, and remind you of what doesn't belong in the course and what does. Table 7.1 shows examples of what course-level essential questions sound like, each with a version the teacher would be thinking about while designing the course and a version to use with students. How you word a question always depends on the age, experiences, and values of your students.

Course-level questions are often simply strand questions—questions that indicate ongoing themes, practices, or assessment tasks in the course—or else they're broader, less interesting versions of unit questions. Unit-based questions like *What makes Steinbeck Steinbeck?* or *How do I score when I shoot?* will probably interest the students

Table 7.1.   Course-Level Essential Questions

Course	Essential Question, Teacher Version: • suggests a course for teaching • reflects the values of the learning community	Essential Question, Student Version: • suggests a course for learning • stimulates students' interest and thinking
English	What strategies can I use to avoid plagiarism and show honesty and integrity in expressing myself?	How do I know my words are mine?
Math	What situations require accuracy, what situations require approximation, and how do we know?	When is "close enough" good enough?
Chemistry	How can I make a reasonable prediction based on qualitative and quantitative data?	How do I know what will happen?
French	What are the grammatical and cultural conventions around using interrogatives and commands in different places where French is spoken?	How can I ask for what I want in an appropriate way?
History	What patterns of behavior do we see in history that resemble patterns of behavior today?	How is now like then?
Music	How does a musician in an ensemble respond to sheet music, the conductor, and other musicians?	Who do I listen to when I play?
Art	How do the properties of materials influence the artist's choices?	What can I make with this?
Physical Education	What are the responsibilities of individual players on a successful team?	What do I need to do to make this a winning team?

and focus the teacher more effectively than the broader versions, *What defines an author's style?* or *How does a player score points?*

Also, course-level questions are often so broad that they encompass entire academic programs. A question like *What defines an author's style?* is one that students could use just as well when reading Eric Carle's picture books in kindergarten as they could when reading Faulkner's novels in a senior seminar. The far reach of a question might mean it contains an important concept, but a question that encompasses an entire discipline can't do much to help a teacher organize a single course. What can?

DESIGNING A MEANINGFUL ASSESSMENT MIX

An assessment mix is the variety of ways your students make their understandings visible. If writing a value-dense assessment is akin to choosing nutritious orange juice over an equal amount of soda, creating a values-congruent assessment mix for your entire course is like choosing a nutritionally balanced diet. Yogurt and broccoli have very different nutritional profiles, so eating one at breakfast and one at lunch helps you fulfill your body's needs for the whole day. A mix of assessment types over the year will serve different values at different times.

Just as your body needs more from certain food groups than others, your course might need more of certain assessment types than others to serve your values. A Chinese teacher might give weekly spoken quizzes if he values oral fluency and wants his students to assess their own and each others' pronunciation and vocabulary. If he also values serving the community, he might have his students translate school documents or local information guides for Chinese-speaking families. This service-learning project might happen only once a year but still be enough to serve values.

Textbox 7.1 offers a protocol you can use to examine your assessment mix and potentially adjust it. The protocol includes directions for using it alone and with colleagues. When you're brainstorming possible assessment tasks for your course, you can refer back to the list of assessment types (textbox 5.1).

MORE FACTORS IN CREATING AN ASSESSMENT MIX

Beyond thinking about what types of tasks students can perform to demonstrate their learning, you might also consider your assessment mix in terms of:

Media

You might give assessments that by definition require particular media; for example, making an oil painting requires paints, canvas, palette, and brushes. And you might give an assessment, like a dance performance or spoken quiz, that can be accomplished with no materials at all. An increasing number of assessments involve electronic media: Students take tests and write papers on computers or tablets, and they use various software apps to make images, audio recordings, presentations, and movies.

TEXTBOX 7.1

EXAMINING AN ASSESSMENT MIX

Times in this protocol are approximate. Depending on how many people are participating and how much you've discussed assessment practices in the past, you might need significantly more or less time. You might do the two parts of this protocol over multiple days.

PART 1: ARTICULATING VALUES IN ASSESSMENT PRACTICES (60 MINUTES)

1. List all the assessment types you *could* use to see and measure what your students know and can do. These might be assessment tasks you already use, have used in the past, or can imagine using, given what you know about your students and subject.

2. Individually, write down some notes about how each assessment type in your list might serve your individual and collective values. Some of these questions might help:

   - How would this task be a worthwhile use of the students' time?

   - How could this assessment help show what the students learned?

   - If my students could complete this task, what would they be able to do next?

   - Why might we choose to assess our students in this particular way?

   - Which values would this assessment task serve?

3. Share responses with the group. The group says back what you seem to be valuing in assessment practices.

4. If you're working with colleagues who teach the same subject or grade level, listen carefully for where you are serving similar values through different assessment practices and where similar assessment practices might be serving different values.

PART 2: FINDING A VALUES-CONGRUENT MIX OF ASSESSMENT TYPES (60 MINUTES)

1. Write how many of each assessment task you've identified as important you think your students should do throughout their experience in your program. Consider your own values as well as how standards, school mission, and school culture create expectations around types and numbers of assessments.

TEXTBOX 7.1. *(Continued)*

2. Now that you have a number for each assessment type, take that number of sticky notes and write the assessment type on each one. (For example, if you said your students should write four lab reports during seventh-grade science, take four sticky notes and write "lab report" on each one.) Make as many sticky notes as you need for each assessment type. It might help to use different colored sticky notes for different assessment types.

3. Write out the names of all your units on chart paper. Distribute assessments by putting the sticky notes next to units.

4. If the assessment you currently give for a unit doesn't match the assessment type you've placed with that unit, consider changing the assessment. If you're working with a colleague, discuss the pros and cons of making that change.

The media students use will depend on availability and cost as well as the teacher's familiarity with the media and capacity to teach students how to use them. Media will also create and remove valued possibilities. For example, designing a "house of the future" using software enables students to revise their plans easily and share them widely, but using cardboard gives students the physical stimulation and immediate feedback provided by handwork. Over time, the teacher might design an assessment mix where students do some projects using software and others using cardboard.

Group Size

Most assessments can be completed by individual students, pairs, or groups. Again, the size of the group will create problems and possibilities. A larger group allows for more perspectives and ideas, but it also gives room for some students to take over, slack off, or have their ideas drowned out by their more assertive peers.

Locations

"Homework" is sometimes an assessment students complete at home, though not all homework serves the function of making understanding visible. Some homework gives students extra practice in a skill or familiarizes them with content they'll explore more deeply in class. Many assessments happen over time, with some of the work completed in class and some at home. Tests usually happen in class, but not always, and some assessments can only happen in a particular location, like a cooking demonstration done in a school kitchen or a physics lab done on an amusement park field trip.

Stakes

Some labels for assessments reflect how much it counts—toward a student's final grade, placement in a future course, or other reward. Calling something a quiz, test, or exam usually tells the student more about the stakes of the assessment than what the task will entail. Some teachers use point systems to let their students know the stakes of an assessment: a high-stakes project might be worth 100 points while a lower-stakes quiz might be worth 20.

CHARTING AN ASSESSMENT MIX

Once you've designed your assessment mix, you can chart it out so you have it for future reference, analysis, and reevaluation. Table 7.2 shows what an assessment mix chart might look like. The different kinds of information on the chart shows just some ways to think about how an assessment mix can serve values; your chart can have as many or as few categories as make sense for you.

You might think of your own ways to classify assessments to help you see what matters to you. Since this chart is for an English class—where most student compositions are written and most performances are *also* written because real-world practitioners of the discipline are writers—the categories of "composition" and "performance" don't show the teacher where her value of encouraging effective written communication is served. A teacher who values hands-on experiential education might be interested in how many of his assessments require engineering—making, testing, and fixing things.

In examining your assessment mix, you might think it's best to expose students to a variety of tasks, or you might give them a steady diet of one or two task types to help them master the skills involved. Variety and exposure versus consistency and mastery are just more values for you to consider.

SEQUENCING YOUR COURSE

Ayanna teaches sixth-grade American history and eighth-grade world cultures and geography. If she's asked about what she does in her courses, she says that in sixth grade, she goes from the Revolutionary War to the civil rights movement. Then she takes a deep breath and explains that in eighth grade, she "goes by region," with units on Latin America, Africa, Europe, and Asia. At the end of the year, each student chooses a country to study in greater depth and does a project, culminating in "World Day" every June.

In her American history course, Ayanna doesn't think too much about sequence; she teaches the content in the order in which it happened. But the geography course—like

Table 7.2. Assessment Mix Chart for a Course
Course: English 7

Unit	Assignment	Type	Modality	Technology	Group Size	Location	Stakes
Coming-of-Age Stories	Photo essay on what it means to come of age	Composition	Visual	Camera	Individual	Home	Medium
	Essay on coming of age	Composition	Written	Computer	Individual	School/Home	High
Poetry with Purpose	Collection of five poems on a single topic	Performance	Written	Computer	Individual	School/Home	High
	Recording for class poetry CD	Performance	Spoken	Audio recording app	Individual	School	Medium
Reinventing Shakespeare	Shakespeare passage recitation	Performance	Spoken	None	Group	School	Medium
	Essay on how setting affects a play's meaning	Composition	Written	Computer	Individual	School/Home	High
Imagining Success	Essay describing a neighborhood "success story"	Performance	Written	Computer	Individual	School/Home	High
	2D artwork to accompany the essay	Composition	Visual	Paper, ink, paint, glue, etc.	Individual	Home	Low
What Success Means to Me	Vignette collection	Performance	Written	Computer	Individual	School/Home	High
Becoming an Activist	Essay describing an award based on an activist	Composition	Written	Computer	Individual	School/Home	High
Activism Takes the Stage	Physical representation of the award	Composition	Visual	Assorted	Individual	Home	Low
	Dramatic scene about an injustice	Performance	Written	Computer	Group	School/Home	High
TOTALS	Assignments—12	Composition—6 Performance—6	Written—7 Spoken—2 Visual—3	Electronic—9 Analog—3	Individual—10 Group—2	Home—3 School—2 Both—7	High—7 Medium—3 Low—2

most courses—doesn't have an inherent order. Nothing about Latin America makes the fall an ideal time for studying it. The students don't need a foundational understanding of Latin American physical and cultural geography in order to learn about Africa. Latin America doesn't even come first in the textbook; the class skips around. "World Day" could just as logically start the course as end it.

Course sequences are not fixed or intrinsic to the subject matter. Even history courses have no "natural" order; just because history happened in an order doesn't mean it must be taught in that order. Science teachers don't teach their content in the order in which it was discovered, and music isn't taught according to when it was composed. Course sequences are constructs rooted in the values of those who make them.

A course's sequence is often a matter of tradition. A unit might be associated with a particular time of year, like a fall unit on farms that coincides with the harvest, a winter music unit that features holiday songs, or a spring P.E. unit on baseball. Some course traditions seem arbitrary: "Fifth graders have always done Egypt at the end of the year." Though Ayanna's geography course skips around the textbook, many courses do follow textbook sequences.

Sequencing units because that's how they've been sequenced in a textbook or by tradition isn't bad; it's just not the only possibility for your course, and there might be a different sequence of units that will better move your students in a valued direction. Here are some factors you might consider when you're putting your units in an order.

Creating Balance between Competing Values

If you have deeply held values that seem to clash, you can create balance between them. An English teacher who values the community built through shared experiences as well as individual choice could use some whole-class texts and some student-chosen texts. When you're sequencing your course, you might alternate between units that serve different values or move gradually from one pole toward the other. Alternating between whole-class and individual-choice text units could make sense, though it could also make sense to create a reading community early in the year and gradually give students more choice in their reading as the year goes on.

Building on Students' Existing Knowledge and Skill Sets

Many teachers sequence their courses such that the early units establish foundational knowledge and skills that later units build on, like how math teachers build on students' knowledge of geometry when they introduce trigonometric functions, or how first-grade teachers build on their students' ability to read fiction when they introduce informational texts. When you're sequencing your units, you might cluster those that demand similar skills so students have a chance to practice these skills intensively, or you might spread these units out so students regularly return to the skills and don't forget them.

Creating a Progression of Ideas

In a single unit, essential questions direct your and your students' attention to important ideas. Over several units, or even your entire course, a series of essential questions can show students how these ideas build on each other.

After revising her Steinbeck unit to focus on how his texts question definitions of success, Allison revised and resequenced three more units to help her students develop an even deeper understanding of what success means. The essential questions for these units are:

- *What does it mean to be successful? Who gets to be successful?* (Unit text: *Of Mice and Men*)
- *How do we define success for ourselves?* (Unit text: *The House on Mango Street*)
- *How do activists help make sure everyone has a chance to be successful? What does it take to be an activist?* (Unit text: choice of activist memoirs)
- *How can I use my writing as a form of activism?* (Unit text: *A Raisin in the Sun*)

Notice that the words *success* and *activism* deliberately echo through the essential questions to help students see how the ideas in these units build upon each other. The wording of your essential questions can draw attention to important ideas that reappear throughout your course. Then, if you sequence your units to create a meaningful progression of ideas, your students will be more likely to see that progression.

Upcycling Student Work

"Upcycling" involves using something old and worn out (like the tweed jacket your grandfather wore in the 1970s) as raw materials to make something new and better (like a cute purse for your daughter). The term was coined by designers William McDonough and Michael Braungart, whose books *Cradle to Cradle* (2002) and *The Upcycle* (2013) describe how to design not just for sustainability but for improvement.

Though practically all teachers make use of prior knowledge and experience—like when a math teacher builds on students' understanding of integers in a subsequent unit on equations—teachers rarely make use of past work products. More often, students take their work home to be displayed, filed, and eventually thrown out.

Instead, the products of student learning from one unit can be upcycled in a future unit. When Laurie teaches her unit on *The Absolutely True Diary of a Part-Time Indian*, her students write short stories about how their identities conflict with each other or with the world around them. Later in the year, during a unit on graphic novels, these students use a graphic format to depict key moments from their identity-in-conflict stories.

If you're willing to think creatively with your colleagues, you might even find opportunities for students to use what they made in one class as materials to upcycle in another class. For example, students could grow vegetables in science and use them when they do cooking demonstrations in their language classes. They could upcycle graphs from a math class into collages in art. They could write poems in English and turn them into performance pieces in drama.

Upcycling work from class to class doesn't necessarily require the teachers involved to share goals. If a student creates a video for P.E. to display her progress in softball, she fulfills the valued purpose of the assessment when she makes, presents, and regularly reviews the video. Later, in science class, this student might add equations and commentary to her video to describe the motion of the ball during different at-bats. The P.E. and science teachers might have totally different goals in their respective courses, but together they create an opportunity for the student to upcycle her work product from one class to another.

If students see that the things they create for your course can be upcycled, perhaps they'll find that their work products and the processes of making them feel more worthwhile. Upcycling also gives students an authentic reason to reassess their creations, refine their thinking, and bring new and better ideas into their work. What do your students make? How could they upcycle these work products as meaningful parts of later units? How could you take advantage of your unit sequence—or how could you resequence your units—so students can upcycle their work from one unit to the next?

THINKING FLEXIBLY ABOUT SEQUENCE

If your course follows a textbook or a long-standing tradition, it might be difficult to imagine any other way to sequence it. Textbox 7.2 has a protocol to help you reimagine the order of your units in light of your values. You can do most of it by yourself, but getting a colleague's perspective will probably help you think more critically and creatively. You might choose to work with a colleague who teaches in your subject area or grade level, or you might think more flexibly (and speak more freely) if your partner doesn't have the same sort of investment in your curriculum as you do.

ASSESSING YOUR COURSE

If aligning a unit is challenging, aligning a course is even more so. How do you know if your course is working as a meaningful system? A great way to discover the extent to which your course matches your values is to get your students' feedback, either in informal "How was that for you?" conversations or through more formal course evaluations. Your school might put out course evaluations keyed to administrative priorities, but you can also make your own, keyed to your values.

For example, if it's important to you that students feel a sense of belonging, you could ask them, "Where did you see yourself in the material you learned this year?" If

TEXTBOX 7.2

UNIT SEQUENCING PROTOCOL

For this protocol, you need a partner who will listen to your ideas about unit sequencing and give you feedback. If your partner is also working on unit sequencing, then after working through this protocol you can switch roles and start over from the beginning. Times are approximate.

1. Write the valued focus of each unit on a sticky note. You might include other relevant information, like the assessment or a resource you use, but make sure the thing you value most draws your eye. (10 minutes)

2. Arrange the sticky notes so your units in an order other than the order they're in now. You might consider: (10 minutes)

   - Ways to balance competing values
   - Ways to build on students' knowledge and skills from one unit to the next
   - Ways to create conceptual arcs
   - Ways to upcycle work products from one unit to the next

3. Explain to your partner why you put the units in the new order. Try your best not to make statements about why the order is or isn't better than the order you currently use or why the order would or wouldn't work. Just say why you put them in this order. Your partner takes notes on what you say. (10 minutes)

4. Optional: If you're willing and interested, put the units in yet another order that's different from the one you traditionally use, and explain the logic of the order. (10 minutes)

5. Put the units in the order they're in now and explain to your partner why they're in this order. Again, try your best to explain the order without judging it as better, worse, necessary, etc. (10 minutes)

6. Ask your partner to say back to you what you seem to be valuing by putting the units in each order. Take notes. (10 minutes)

you want them to learn transferable skills, you could ask, "What did you learn in this class that you used in other classes or outside school?" Any course evaluation could include the question, "What do you think the point of this course was?" Students' responses to these kinds of prompts will show you where you've succeeded in teaching by your values and where your course might need work.

Another way to assess your course is to make a values map. Perhaps teachers at your school already make curriculum maps: documents showing what happens in academic programs. Just as geographic maps can have all kinds of purposes—from aviation charts that help pilots navigate from the air to road maps that show features drivers need—different maps of your curriculum can serve different functions. A map intended to communicate to students and families about your school's academic program will look quite different from a map made to show you the extent to which you're teaching by your values.

Curriculum mapping can become a time-consuming process, but maps should include only the information and level of detail they need to serve their purpose. If you wanted to show your mother-in-law how to get your kids from your house to the local playground, a rough map drawn in thirty seconds would serve its purpose just as well as if you took an hour to add detail. A values map, too, should be only as detailed as necessary to serve its purposes.

Textbox 7.3 is a map of Allison's seventh-grade English course that she made to see where her value of promoting student choice manifests itself. The map isn't long or detailed, but it illuminates something this teacher genuinely values and wants to work on. She didn't make this map to follow an administrative mandate; she made it so she could help herself teach by her values.

Looking at the map, Allison might notice that the units in the middle of the year involve less choice than the units at the beginning and end. Maybe she should add more choice to one of her mid-year units as a way to defeat her students' winter blahs. Or maybe she should move her units around so they alternate between those with lots of choice and those with less. She could incorporate more choice into units where her students are less excited about the book or the project. She could show this map to some colleagues or former students and see what they think. Or she could decide her students already have just the right amount of choice during the year.

To make your own values map, simply write down the names of all the units you teach, and for each unit, jot down all the ways one of your values manifests itself. Also write down any strands where your value shows up. Notice what stands out. Do you see any patterns in when or how your value manifests itself? What's puzzling or problematic? Now that you've made visible where in your course you can find something

TEXTBOX 7.3

VALUES MAP OF A COURSE

Course: English 7
Value: Student Choice
Units:

First Trimester	Second Trimester	Third Trimester
Coming-of-Age Stories (various novels about coming of age) • which coming-of-age book to read • aspect of coming of age to write about in the essay Poetry with Purpose • topic for original poetry collection • which original poems to use in the collection • which original poem to read for the class CD Reinventing Shakespeare (*A Midsummer Night's Dream*) • where to reimagine the play's setting	Imagining Success (*Of Mice and Men*) • essay topic • type of art that accompanies the essay What Success Means to Me (*The House on Mango Street*) • vignette topics	Becoming an Activist (memoirs by activists) • which activist memoir to read • who to give the award to Activism Takes the Stage (*A Raisin in the Sun*) • topic of dramatic scene students write • how to fictionalize the real-life conflict • members of the collaborative writing group • group norms • how the work will be divided

Strands:

Writing to Think

- what to write about

Revision

- which strategies to use for revision
- which peer(s) read their work and give them feedback

Grammar Toolkit

- whether and how to incorporate new grammar tools into the writing you value, you can make decisions about what to do next: what you want to add, cut, change, rearrange, and leave alone in order to serve your values more effectively.

In the process of assessing your course, perhaps you've identified a values dilemma you're having trouble resolving, or you want to take your course in some valued direction but aren't sure how. Now would be a good time to call upon your colleagues for some perspective. If you bring a values dilemma to a group of your colleagues, even if they don't solve all your problems, the act of listening to others wrestle with ways to make your course more values-congruent can be clarifying and can build the kinds of relationships that will allow for continued work together.

8

Optimizing Your Students' Experience

How can you use your values to identify gaps and overloads, and what can a teacher do about them?

Natural systems maintain "just right" amounts of what they need. Your body keeps its temperature at about 98.6 degrees. If you go running, the sweat evaporating from your skin cools you down, and if you dive into cold water, your shivering warms you up. Hawks keep a chipmunk population stable, which means the chipmunks have enough nuts and seeds to eat. As long as a natural system doesn't have to absorb too much of something (like carbon or garbage), the system self-regulates so it has the optimal amount of whatever it needs.

Unlike a natural system that regulates itself, a curriculum must be constructed to have the "just right" amounts of what students need, according to values and within the constraints of the school schedule, calendar, physical space, budget, and staffing. You probably have opinions about whether the curriculum has "just right" amounts of things you value: "These kids need twice as much art and half as many tests" or, "Why can't our school have a gardening program?" or, to quote Sir Ken Robinson (2006), "There isn't an education system on the planet that teaches dance every day to children the way we teach them mathematics. Why?"

Most teachers have little if any say in how the larger academic program looks, and like any single actor within a system, you have only so much impact. Still, your choices do matter: You might have some agency over the course you teach, and you can talk to your colleagues and administrators about the curriculum in your subject area and grade level. This chapter is about how to optimize your course within the context of the larger systems to which it belongs.

GAPS IN THE CURRICULUM

Can you think of any topics, concepts, skill sets, or practices that matter to you but seem underrepresented in the curriculum—or that are missing entirely?

Maybe you think your students don't move their bodies enough, or engage in enough imaginative play, or build enough things with their hands. Maybe you think your students don't learn enough about recent historical events, or study enough grammar, or learn enough about art or science. Maybe you feel your program focuses too much on academic skills and not enough on social skills. Maybe you think none of these things, because "not enough" according to one person's values might be "enough" or even "too much" according to another's.

Even when a curricular element is widely valued at a school, some content, skills, and assessment types get treated as the province of a particular department or grade level. If the civil rights movement is a fourth grade topic, other grades might avoid it—even if it's relevant to their courses and even if fourth graders don't learn all there is to learn about it. The Common Core places writing within the domain of social studies and science, but students still might do most of their writing in English class. Teachers of history and science, or math and music, might not think it's their responsibility to teach writing or know how to create writing-based assessment tasks.

MAKING A VALUES MAP OF A PROGRAM

One way to find gaps in your subject-area or grade-level curriculum is to make a values map that includes all the courses in it. Table 8.1 shows an example of what a programmatic values map could look like. This map is of an eighth-grade program and shows how the values of cooperation and collaboration manifest themselves.

This particular values map is laid out as a monthly chart so it can show which classes use collaborative methods and where in the year these collaborations fall. The map suggests that language units contain the most group work, which perhaps makes sense, since language use is social, and that music and P.E. have the most frequent collaboration in strands, which also makes sense since kids play team sports and make music as an ensemble.

Teachers in a department or team who have similar values could work together to make a map like this and use it to help them make decisions. The eighth-grade teachers who give less group work might consider ways to give more, or they might decide that their students work together enough in other classes and also need time to think and learn as individuals. The teachers might decide to spread out the collaborative work, since some months are full of group projects while others have hardly any, or perhaps they'll see reasons to cluster group projects together. A values map allows the team to decide whether to make revisions and what those revisions should be.

Even if your colleagues won't make or review values maps with you, you can still find gaps in your program by mapping it yourself. Though it might feel a little weird to map other people's courses to your values, you can make decisions about your own course based on what you find in the overall program. For example, if the eighth-grade

Table 8.1. A Programmatic Values Map
Grade: 8
Value: Cooperation/collaboration
In Units:

	Sept.	Oct.	Nov.	Dec.	Jan.	Feb.	Mar.	Apr.	May
English		Lord of the Flies trial				Romeo and Juliet trial			Interviews for "Religion in Our Lives" project
History		Ancient Egyptian roleplay		Video on connections between Ancient Rome and today					
Language: Chinese	Farmers market simulation		"Friends at My House" movie	House rental advertisement project		Write a song about seeing a doctor		Buying clothes roleplay	School emergency skits
Language: French	Skits about introducing oneself	Shopping skits	Phone conversation skits					French-speaking country poster project	Class play
Language: Spanish	Grammar review board game			Market stall simulation		Navigating school scavenger hunt	Childhood memories interview project	Debate on current events	Cooking shows
Math				Graphing systems of equations project					
Science	Bridge project			Making a catapult		Mousetrap car project			Journal article peer review

Table 8.1. (*continued*)
In strands:

Strands		At Least Once per Class	At Least Once per Week	At Least Once per Unit	Occasionally during the Year
English	Book partners		X	X	
	Peer review of writing				
History	Small group analysis of historical events		X		X
	Critical assessment of fellow students' work				
Languages	Partner conversations		X		X
	Group songs				
Math	Problem-solving groups	X	X		
	Solution-checking pairs				
Music	Playing/singing as an ensemble	X			
PE	Working as a team	X			
	Fair and appropriate conduct	X			
Science	Lab partnerships			X	

history teacher made this map herself, she might decide to move her group project about Rome from December, when there's lots of group work going on in other classes, to January when there's none. If there's "not enough" of something valued in the curriculum, you might be able to put more of it into your course.

REPETITIONS IN THE CURRICULUM

Your school probably has repeating units, like a P.E. unit on basketball every winter in high school, or a holiday concert where all middle school music students perform, or a unit on geometry as part of each year in elementary school math. You might also find strands that run through multiple grades, like lab safety in science, current events in history, or color studies in art. These kinds of repetitions might serve school values and create a more coherent experience that helps the students retain important learning. Or the repetitions might just be repetitive.

Before you can decide whether curricular repetitions serve values, you first have to find them, and repetitions can be even harder to spot than gaps. Areas that are underemphasized or missing entirely will bump up against your values—students won't be able to add or spell or think critically, and that will drive you crazy—but overemphasis isn't as apparent. You might notice it within your own course ("Does anything significant happen in history without there being a war?!"), but you probably won't notice repetitions throughout your school unless you really look.

One way to find repetitions is to look in curriculum maps for similar units popping up from year to year. Perhaps you'll find that every year of English includes a poetry unit, or that every science course begins with a unit on the scientific method, or that every ninth-grade course includes a research project in February. The problem with using a curriculum map to find repetitions is that it needs to be clear and thorough enough to make those repetitions visible. Mapping that thoroughly could take a lot of your and your colleagues' time, and you won't know when you've put in enough information until you see the repetitions, if they exist at all.

Another potential problem with using maps is that teachers might phrase similar ideas in different ways, and an observer might not recognize repetitions as such. If the first units of sixth-, seventh-, and eighth-grade science were called "Observation and Inference," "Being a Scientist," and "Process Skills," the teachers might not realize that all three units are reviews of the scientific method.

If you can't find repetitions by looking in curriculum maps, you might find them by listening to your students. They might just tell you about curricular repetitions (though not necessarily in the tone of voice you'd prefer): "We're building model cars again? We did that in fifth grade!" You could also ask students if there's anything they feel like they're always learning about, to their boredom or exhaustion, or even to their pleasure. It's not necessarily bad if your students learn about war after war in history or if they're building model cars in multiple grades, but it's worth knowing so you can decide if that repetition is values-congruent.

Another good resource for finding repetitions is any adult associated with your school but not your specific program. Parents might be willing to answer questions like, "What did it seem like your children were always doing in their math classes?" or "What do you see as the emphasis in music classes at this school?" You can ask a colleague in another department something like, "Have you ever noticed patterns in the way we teach languages here?" or someone who teaches another grade a question like, "From where you're standing, what seems central in second grade?"

Conversations like these might feel awkward; some adults would rather say nothing than say something that could be perceived as critical, and others might take your questions as an invitation to lob grenades at your program—or even at your colleagues and you! Still, adults in your community might have lots of helpful observations to share, so perhaps these risks are worthwhile. If you do find repetitions, you can decide if they're meaningful—in which case, you can emphasize the interconnections in your program when you teach—or if they're merely repetitive.

If you find repetitions in your program, note that similar units don't necessarily mean those who teach them have similar values. In a phenomenon known as homoplasy, organisms look similar even though they don't share an ancestor, like how the rhinoceros and triceratops both have tank-like bodies and big nose horns but aren't closely related. That might not matter—both animals benefit from their sturdiness and horns, and students will benefit from learning geometry even if their teachers value it for different reasons—but if you start talking to colleagues about repetitions in your program, the values underlying these units will inevitably begin to affect your discussions.

OPTIMIZING THE CURRICULUM

If you think your program has "too much" or "too little" of something, you can work with your department or team to decide what "just right" looks like, given your students' characteristics and your collective values. Instead of framing your inquiry as one seeking deficits and overloads (and thus putting yourself and your colleagues on the defensive), you can discuss ways a particular element of the curriculum serves values. For example, a group of teachers examining independent reading could ask questions like:

- How is independent reading a worthwhile use of our students' time?
- Why might we ask our students to do independent reading?
- Which of our values would independent reading serve?
- If our students do enough independent reading, what will they be able to do next?
- What would doing a lot of independent reading keep students from doing?

Once you and your colleagues have talked about your values related to a particular skill, process, content area, theme, instructional method, assessment type, or other element of the curriculum, you can ask some variation of, "How much of this should our students be doing during a particular time period?" Some examples of discussion questions are:

- How much independent reading should fourth graders do during the week?
- How much do ninth graders need to move their bodies during their school day?
- How many sixth grade assignments should involve the arts?
- How many middle school math assessments should be tests?
- How many history classes should begin the year with general foundation or review?
- How many projects should students have due right before major school vacations?

In addition to values, you'll need to consider how standards, school mission and culture, and your students' needs create expectations around this element of the curriculum.

Once you've established an optimal amount of what students "should do," you and your colleagues can develop a coordinated plan for how to distribute the curricular element across your classes. For example, the teachers of sixth-grade history, science, math, and English could work together to decide how many art-based assignments belong in each class. They might distribute art-based assignments evenly across their classes, or they might put more art in some classes than others.

PROGRAMMATIC ASSESSMENT MIXES

If you're considering your course's assessment mix—the variety of ways students display their learning—remember that your students are taking (or will take) other courses, too. Working with your colleagues who teach these courses, you can optimize the mix of assessments across the classes in your subject area or grade level.

If you talk to your colleagues about assessments in your subject or grade, you might discover that your students do similar tasks from class to class. That might be helpful: Grant Wiggins and Jay McTighe (2007, 82–83) advocate for similar assessment tasks to recur throughout a program, with appropriate increases in the task's sophistication and in the students' expected capabilities.

For example, a recurring assessment task in science could involve collecting, displaying, and interpreting data. Kindergartners might observe and draw bean plants and then spend circle time discussing why some plants have more flowers than others. Though this scene looks very different from goggled tenth graders using a spectrophotometer to measure the concentrations of chemicals in a solution and writing lab reports about their findings, both classes are collecting, displaying, and interpreting data. A piano student might give a recital every year but play increasingly difficult pieces, from "Twinkle

Twinkle Little Star" to Beethoven's *Waldstein* sonata, with increasing technical perfection and personal style.

On the other hand, similar assessment tasks within a discipline or grade might just mean that two teachers independently thought of or found the same idea without realizing it. A popular assignment in middle-grade writing classes is to use George Ella Lyon's poem "Where I'm From" as a model for students' own "Where I'm From" poems. You can probably imagine a fifth-grade English teacher asking his students to collect images from their childhoods to write their own "Where I'm From" poems while his colleague down hall has the same students collect images of Revolutionary War figures to write "Where I'm From" poems about them.

Given how easy the internet makes finding assessment ideas, it's not all that unlikely that you and a colleague will come across the same one and want to use it in your respective courses. As teachers of the same subject or students, you might read the same magazines, subscribe to the same newsletters, or check the same websites.

As you work on your course's assessment mix, you'll probably want to communicate with your colleagues. That way, instead of accidentally giving students the same assessment tasks in multiple courses—or missing opportunities to create meaningful task progressions—you can deliberately give similar or varied assessments within your program.

Tables 8.2 and 8.3 show examples of programmatic assessment mix charts. These charts represent compiled data from English courses and seventh-grade courses from a middle school. It includes the English 7 course charted in table 7.2.

REMOVING BARRIERS TO OPTIMIZING THE CURRICULUM

As you and your colleagues work on optimizing your curriculum, you might find some people saying students need something—like movement or art or grammar instruction—but hesitating to claim it for their own classes.

If you notice your colleagues who value a practice expressing their barriers to using it in statements like, "There's no place for movement in a calculus class," or "I'd best leave the grammar instruction to the English teachers," you can name your own barriers, talk openly about your struggles, and reaffirm your values. You could say something like, "Yeah, I'm not such a grammarian either. I still don't know what a preposition is. But if I want the kids to write clearer lab reports, then I'll do what I can to help them." If you want your colleagues to be willing to make themselves vulnerable, it helps if you go first.

Shared professional development experiences around a mutually valued practice can help, too. The members of your department or team could all read an article, attend a workshop together, visit the classes of those at your school who have expertise in the area, or ask these experts to train the rest of you through a simulated class. These

Table 8.2. Assessment Mix Chart for an Academic Program: English 6–8

Grade	Number of Major Assessments	Assignment Types	Modalities	Group Size
6	10	Composition - 4 Performance - 4 Case Study - 2 Test - 0	Written - 7 Spoken - 3 Visual - 1	Individual - 9 Pair - 0 Group - 1
7	12	Composition - 6 Performance - 6 Case Study - 0 Test - 0	Written - 7 Spoken - 2 Visual - 3	Individual - 10 Pair - 1 Group - 1
8	14	Composition - 6 Performance - 6 Case Study - 2 Test - 0	Written - 11 Spoken - 2 Visual - 1	Individual - 12 Pair - 0 Group - 2
TOTALS	36	Composition - 18 Performance - 15 Case Study - 3 Test - 0	Written - 26 Spoken - 5 Visual - 5	Individual - 30 Pair - 1 Group - 5

Table 8.3. Assessment Mix Chart for an Academic Program: 7th Grade

Subject	Number of Major Assessments	Assignment Types	Modalities	Group Size
English	12	Composition - 6 Performance - 6 Case Study - 0 Test - 0	Written - 7 Spoken - 2 Visual - 3	Individual - 10 Pair - 1 Group - 1
History	11	Composition - 2 Performance - 2 Case Study - 2 Test - 5	Written - 7 Spoken - 3 Visual - 1	Individual - 6 Pair - 5 Group - 0
Math	11	Composition - 0 Performance - 1 Case Study - 2 Test - 8	Written - 10 Spoken - 1 Visual - 0	Individual - 8 Pair - 0 Group - 3
Science	14	Composition - 4 Performance - 2 Case Study - 2 Test - 6	Written - 7 Spoken - 4 Visual - 3	Individual - 10 Pair - 2 Group - 2
TOTALS	48	Composition - 12 Performance - 11 Case Study - 6 Test - 19	Written - 31 Spoken - 10 Visual - 7	Individual - 34 Pair - 8 Group - 6

experiences lower external barriers and increase willingness to act in spite of internal barriers. You and your colleagues will also have a reference point to hold each other accountable ("Have you done any of those movement activities we learned about? How are they going?").

These shared experiences ultimately are ways to build respect and empathy for each other, grow in a mutually valued direction, and ultimately create the professional community you need if you want to keep writing a more cohesive and meaningful curriculum for your students.

VALUES CONFLICTS

The process of examining your course within its subject area and grade level curriculum can give rise to conflict even when you and your colleagues share values. You might disagree on the amount of time to devote to a practice you all value or on the best ways to implement that valued practice. How do you and your colleagues optimize your students' experience if your values themselves are fundamentally different?

Eva is a ninth-grade Spanish teacher. Valuing communication and cultural competency in the real world, she arranges field trips to Spanish-speaking areas so her students can use Spanish to do everyday tasks like buying lunch and asking for directions. Eva finds that the kids don't need perfect grammar in order to communicate in the real world. Her colleague Martin, who teaches tenth-grade Spanish, values accuracy in communication. To Martin, true fluency involves using correct grammar so his students aren't stumbling along saying "I go" when they mean "I'm going." He gives daily review exercises and weekly oral quizzes on grammar.

Both teachers believe they're right and the other is wrong. Both have read professional articles and heard at professional workshops that the ways they're teaching are "best practices." Each has tried unsuccessfully to convince the other of the merits of his or her approach. Department meetings are tense, and the students see their teachers as trying to undermine each other and are confused about what's important in speaking Spanish. Martin and Eva treat each other with begrudging tolerance and occasional out-in-the-open antagonism, both continuing to think, in effect, "My way is better."

But one approach isn't *better* than the other, like a spoon isn't better than a fork. One approach might better fulfill a particular purpose, like how a fork is better than a spoon for eating salad, but eating salad isn't a better goal than eating soup. You can keep following this logic: Salad or soup might better fulfill a particular purpose, but neither meal is inherently "better" than the other. Follow any goal far enough, and eventually you'll get to values. If it's a cold day and you value comfort, you might go with cream of mushroom soup and use the spoon, and if you value your health, you might choose kale salad and use the fork.

After a nasty and embarrassing argument in the hallway one afternoon, Martin and Eva finally decide to sit down together to try to resolve their conflict. Martin shares that before coming to their school, he tutored high school students from a wide variety of geographic, socioeconomic, and racial backgrounds. About the only thing his tutees had in common was that they all wanted to get into good colleges but struggled to do well in their classes and on standardized tests. Martin now wants to make sure his tenth graders master the grammar they need to be successful going forward.

Eva's background is quite different: She's been teaching Spanish for many years and has corrected thousands of grammatical errors on tests with little effect on her students' ability to communicate in the real world. She wants her students to let the purpose of their speaking guide them and to sound more authentic—more like neighborhood talk than just-for-school talk. Martin believes just-for-school talk is most important because that's the work students will be graded and tested on, and those grades and test scores will affect their futures.

As they continue their conversation, Martin and Eva realize that their different approaches to teaching Spanish stem from their different experiences, but that underneath are some of the same values. They both want their students to develop fluency in Spanish, and they both want their students' use of Spanish to transfer beyond their classes so they'll be successful in the future. Understanding these common values helps Martin and Eva diffuse the tension and proceed from a place of mutual respect.

In class, both Eva and Martin can now articulate how and why their expectations are similar and different. Instead of confusing their students about "what really matters" in speaking a second language—and making them think only one teacher can be right—they now work together to ensure ninth- and tenth-grade Spanish equips students with different but complementary skill sets. Both teachers feel more relaxed around each other from then on, and several students who have been through both of their courses remark on how they feel really solid in their skills.

If your department or team has conflict—whether that conflict has exploded into fighting or is more of a low-grade resentment—you might be able to address it through values clarification. You also might find that one or both colleagues aren't willing or able to do the necessary work to get past the conflict. In situations like these, you can only change your own behavior, so it might help to take a deep breath and refocus yourself on the places where you can act in accordance with your values.

INTEGRATING DIVERSE VALUES

When naturalists use the word "diversity," they're describing the way a wide variety of species creates resilience within an ecosystem. If the red-tailed hawks in a particular area were threatened, the squirrel and chipmunk populations would still be controlled by other birds of prey, foxes, and snakes. If a fungus attacks one species of elm, birds can live in other trees until the elm population recovers. The more biodiversity, the stronger the ecosystem.

When you create multiple paths to the same understandings, your course becomes more resilient. Teaching sixth graders how to choose books might involve book talks, websites, peer recommendations, and a well-stocked classroom library. Teaching first graders how to resolve conflicts might require picture book discussions, roleplays, and class rule-making sessions. If one lesson fails, another might work. James Banks (1997) explains that a one-size-fits-all curriculum won't serve students who bring all kinds of identities into class with them; supporting all learners equitably means having diverse lessons in the curriculum.

Just as a diversity of lessons leads to a unit that reaches more students, a diversity of valued approaches in different classes can lead to a more resilient academic program. If you have multiple goals (like eating soup *and* salad, or communicating in the real world *and* using correct grammar), it's helpful to have tools to help you achieve your various goals. Instead of sending mixed messages to students and letting conflict destroy relationships among colleagues, you can intentionally integrate your diverse approaches into a more resilient curriculum. Here are some ways to do that.

Writing Programmatic Essential Questions

One way to incorporate diverse values into an academic program is to look for larger, shared values and use these to write programmatic essential questions. Martin and Eva share the larger value of fluency, so a shared essential question for their Spanish program could be something like "What linguistic and cultural competencies must a person possess in order to achieve fluency?"—or in kid language, "What makes you fluent?" By working together to emphasize different aspects of what makes someone fluent, these two teachers create a stronger program.

If your department or team is interested in writing programmatic essential questions, you can use the "Finding What's Essential for Groups" protocol (textbox 3.2), using your common area of focus. For Martin and Eva, the area of focus would be "high school Spanish." If they invited in more teachers, they might broaden their focus to "K–12 Spanish" or "high school languages." For grade-level teams who share students, the common area of focus is the students themselves, so their topic could be something like "third-grade relational skills," or more broadly, "third grade."

Mapping Values in the Program

Another way to make values diversity a source of strength is for different teachers to choose values that their colleagues *don't* seem to share and map the ways that value is served throughout the program. If Martin values accuracy, he could map how students learn to communicate with accuracy throughout high school. Martin might discover unexpected places where his value is served. If he works on the map with his department, he might find that his colleagues make different decisions about how to teach accurate communication in light of the information they uncover.

Seeking Multiple Valued Practices

Instead of trying to narrow your department's or team's repertoire to the "best" practices everyone must use, you can work together to seek more practices that help students learn. Rather than asking, "What's the best way to write an essay?" or "What's better: competition or cooperation?" you can ask, "What different ways to write an essay would help our students?" or "How do cooperation and competition help students learn?" You're then positioned to be more deliberate in balancing curricular elements like:

- Structured and unstructured essays
- Individual and group projects
- Improvised and rehearsed performances
- Discussion-based and writing-based classes
- Competitive and cooperative problem solving
- Student-chosen and teacher-assigned topics

Teachers can argue over whose practices are better, or they can offer a variety of experiences and make sure students understand why each one matters and how they all interconnect. You might imagine Martin saying to his class, "Last year, you learned how to communicate in Spanish in the real world. That's one important kind of fluency. Since you have such a strong background in that area, we're going to focus this year on a different kind of fluency: using correct grammar." Even if you and your colleagues keep your curriculum exactly as it is, you all can give your students more explicit messages about how they're getting multiple benefits from your program.

Connecting Disciplines

How can we create cross-disciplinary units that reflect our values?

Connecting ideas across disciplines gives students more opportunities to process information so they can remember and use it. When teachers prioritize cross-disciplinary ideas over discipline-based facts, their students learn to construct meaning instead of being reduced to memorizers and mimics.

Dan Pink (2006) points out that "seeing the big picture, crossing boundaries, and being able to combine disparate pieces into an arresting new whole" (66) is a key skill now that information is so easy to access, but how can students see the big picture when their different classes create so many little ones? How can teachers expect students to make novel connections while building Berlin Walls between subjects? Enter cross-disciplinary curriculum.

FINDING CONNECTIONS

Most academic standards and academic programs are discipline-based, particularly after the elementary grades and often there, too. Even when students stay in the same classroom with the same teacher, their day is often divided into periods or blocks for discipline-based study. Creating units for discipline-based courses is enough of a challenge when there's some sort of curriculum in place—a topic, text, project, or *something* from which to proceed. Crossing disciplines will often involve creating brand new curriculum. Where do you start?

The best place to look for ideas is within existing courses. If you and your colleagues visit each other's classrooms, look at each other's materials, or just discuss your courses, you might discover opportunities for crossing disciplines hidden in plain sight. If you teach multiple subjects, you might find links between them, and if you teach a single subject, you and a colleague might discover a common topic that's been sitting in your curriculum all along. All you need to do is explicitly and meaningfully connect the dots. That's not as easy as it sounds, especially if you and your colleague encounter values differences, but at least it's a starting point.

If you don't find buried treasure in your existing curriculum, an idea for connecting disciplines can come from just about anywhere else. You could study a topic, like the Olympics, in multiple ways, or use a resource—a book, film, speaker, or field trip—in multiple classes. You could choose an issue, like American obesity or sexism in the media, to study through multiple lenses. You could use a skill, like note-taking or public speaking, or a theme, like success or democracy. Ideas can come from one of your courses, your community, your students' lives, current events, or something you happen to see or do.

If you bring an idea for a collaboration your colleagues, it helps to know a little about their courses so you can imagine them coming up with connections, but you also never know what creative ideas people will have if you invite them to think with you. At worst, your colleagues will learn more about your values and interests, and you'll have a new idea for something worthwhile to use just in your own class.

As great as cross-disciplinary units sound, they often don't work or don't last. How can that be? And more importantly, what conditions are necessary for a cross-disciplinary unit to be functional and sustainable?

WHEN GOOD CROSS-DISCIPLINARY EFFORTS GO BAD

Imagine it's a winter Olympics year, and a group of third-grade teachers are ready! In social studies, the students are taking a break from American history to do country studies and make flags. In P.E. they're cutting the fitness unit to have Olympic-like contests such as "mocksled" racing using tied-together scooters. In English they're competing in a "book-o-lympics" to see who can read the most before the games begin. In art they're painting ancient Greek style figures of themselves playing favorite sports or games. In Spanish they're learning words related to winter activities; and in math they're solving word problems about athletes.

In an attempt to connect their various disciplines, this group of teachers fell right into the ringmaster trap. They figured out fun activities that mention the word "Olympics" or loosely relate to some aspect of the games without articulating why the Olympics are important or what third graders should understand about them. Even if some children enjoy mocksledding or painting vases or winning medals in the book-o-lympics, the overall unit lacks the sense of purpose necessary to engender deeper understandings. It's a heap.

Worse, the Olympics unit is taking time away from valued curriculum. Jere Brophy and Janet Alleman (1991) set two criteria for an effective cross-disciplinary unit: Activities should "be educationally significant, ones desirable even if they did not include the integration feature," and the unit should "foster, rather than disrupt or nullify, accomplishment of major goals in each subject area."

In a values-congruent cross-disciplinary unit, the content, skills, and assessments are *already* important. Teachers make minor adjustments so the connections across disciplines are clear, or they replace a unit with one they value equally or more. Playing pretend sports in P.E. class might be fun, but is it more educationally significant than the fitness unit it displaces? In social studies, the country reports disrupt the regularly scheduled curriculum, and whether flag-making fosters the accomplishment of major learning goals in history is questionable at best.

If the third-grade teachers want to plan a unit together, they can begin by identifying a commonly valued purpose. What makes the Olympics worth studying? Perhaps the key understanding is that people from all over the world share an experience through the Olympics, and their essential question could be, *What brings people together?* Or maybe what's important is that great athletes work hard to improve, and the essential question could be, *Why should I work to get better when I'm already good?* Or maybe the question is, *How can we play against each other without rooting against each other?* or *What makes a tradition survive?*

Once the teachers understand the purpose of the Olympics unit, each of them can craft lessons to fit that purpose—and that fit their courses instead of feeling like a detour. The teachers would also need to explain to the students how these lessons relate to that purpose and to material they're learning in other classes. By identifying and sticking to a commonly valued purpose, teachers can make their students' experience more meaningful and coherent, instead of subverting that aim by creating a new heap of unrelated lessons.

CROSS-DISCIPLINARY ESSENTIAL QUESTIONS

A cross-disciplinary essential question directs attention to what's important to multiple learning communities, piques the students' genuine curiosity about multiple disciplines, and focuses all involved teachers so they know what doesn't belong in the unit and what does. Table 9.1 gives examples of what these kinds of questions sound like.

For more examples of cross-disciplinary essential questions, take a look at the Sustainable Schools Project's *Guide to Education for Sustainability* (Cirillo and Hoyler 2011). Since sustainability involves the interconnections between all living and nonliving things in a community, the questions that get students to think about these ideas will cross subject borders.

To write a cross-disciplinary essential question for a collaborative unit, you can bring together the interested members of your team and try the "Finding What's Essential for Groups" protocol (textbox 3.2). Your team can use any topic, resource, skill, process, or theme that you can imagine students learning through multiple disciplines, but when you're each writing and talking about this area of focus, consider it from the perspective of your discipline.

Table 9.1. Cross-Disciplinary Essential Questions

Essential Question, Teacher Version: • suggests a course for teaching in multiple disciplines • reflects the values of multiple learning communities	Essential Question, Student Version: • suggests a course for learning in multiple disciplines • stimulates students' thinking about multiple subjects
How does the structure or shape of an object relate to its intended function or purpose?	Why this shape?
How will the use of a particular device change the subjective experiences and objective outcomes of a process?	How does technology both help and hinder us?
What does it mean to be a critical consumer of information, ideas, and commodities? Why is it important to be critical about our consumption? How can I become a critical consumer?	Do I buy this?
What does sustainable eating look like—on the personal, cultural, economic, social, and ecological levels?	Should I eat this?
When is a traditional or familiar method best, when is it best to use a new or unfamiliar approach, and how do we know?	When is newer better?
How does diversity ensure resilience within a system and help the system and its parts thrive?	How is diversity good for everyone?
How does a change in one part have ripple effects and unintended consequences throughout the system?	How does a small change become a big change?
When must you follow a rule, when should you follow guidelines, and when can you do things however you want?	Do I have to do it this way?
How can sequencing affect outcomes?	Why this order?
How do biological, technological, and social systems use various types of codes to pass information within the system? How does knowing codes give access to a system?	What can you do if you know the code?

If each member of your team teaches multiple subjects (as many elementary grade teachers do), then you might ask each person to think about the area of focus from the perspective of one subject to ensure different disciplines get represented. Once you've generated questions, you can discuss, evaluate, and rewrite them as necessary, and ultimately you'll choose one question, or a cluster of questions, that suggests a course for teaching and learning in each subject and reflects your collective values.

You might not come up with a question that feels right for everyone—or every subject. Not all topics will lend themselves to meaningful cross-disciplinary study, and even those that do won't necessarily work with the curriculum in your grade level. A fifth-grade team that wants to create a cross-disciplinary unit about democracy might find connections to math, but maybe not the math that their fifth graders learn. If some teachers or subjects can't connect to the question, you might consider finding a different one or having only the courses with an authentic connection participate.

USING CROSS-DISCIPLINARY ESSENTIAL QUESTIONS

If your team writes a cross-disciplinary question, you'll use the "student version" across different subjects as a way to focus your students on important connections among multiple subjects. What the question won't do is tell you what's important about the topic within the context of your course. That's why you'll want to write a "teacher version" of the question that's specific to your discipline and that can help you see what does and doesn't belongs in the unit, as it exists in your class.

Table 9.2 shows cross-disciplinary questions meant for students and subject-specific versions of those questions that teachers could use to design curriculum for use in their classes.

In one discipline or many, a unit is still a unit. Once you have an essential question, the tools for planning lessons, writing assessments, and ensuring alignment from chapters 4, 5, and 6 will work for units that cross disciplines. The brainstorming protocol (textbox 4.1), list of assessment types (textbox 5.1), alignment

Table 9.2. Cross-Disciplinary Questions with Associated Subject-Specific Questions

Cross-Disciplinary Question for Students: • suggests a course for learning in multiple disciplines • stimulates students' thinking about multiple subjects	Subject-Specific Questions for Teachers: • suggests a course for teaching in each discipline • reflects the values of multiple learning communities
What can you do if you know the code?	English: *What can teenage characters do because they understand adult codes of behavior? What happens when they refuse to live by these codes?* History: *How did different members of Mesopotamian society live by different codes? How did they all live by a central code of behavior? How did this code create stability in their society?* Languages: *How does knowing another language give access to another culture? How doesn't it?* Math: *How does knowing the "codes" of algebraic algorithms allow us to solve problems more efficiently?* Music: *How do musicians in an ensemble communicate with each other during a performance?* Science: *Why is DNA called a code? How does the code work? What can we do now that we know how the code works?*
Why this shape?	English: *How does an essay's thesis guide its structure?* History: *What does a city's layout tell us about the people living in it?* Languages: *Should I use the preterite or imperfect tense when I talk about the past?* Math: *When do you use fractions and when do you use decimals?* Music: *How does a musical instrument's shape affect its sounds?* Science: *What do the shapes of animal bones tell us about their behaviors?*

template (figure 6.1), and unit self-assessment (textbox 6.1) would be particularly helpful tools.

OVERLY BROAD ESSENTIAL QUESTIONS

A group of fifth-grade teachers discovers that the theme of "change" comes up in every single subject. They get excited about this theme because everything about their students' lives is on the cusp of change: their bodies, their social groups, and even their schools as they prepare to leave elementary and go to middle. The fifth-grade team comes up with the essential question *How do things change?* and meets again to decide where in the year their "change" unit should go.

The English teacher says she can use this question at any time because her class can study how a character changes in any book they read. The history teacher says his students can examine changes in American society that led to or resulted from any of the events they study, and the science teacher says her kids spend the entire year learning about changes in plants, bodies of water, and biomes. In math, the students can look at how changes in numerical patterns affect the shape of corresponding graphs, and in both P.E. and music, the students can examine how small changes to form affect the quality of their performance.

Cross-disciplinary themes are the biggies that recur throughout history. It's no surprise, then, if these themes pop up throughout all the courses in your grade level—and every grade level! Remember that one purpose of essential questions is to help teachers decide what to include in the unit and what to leave out. A question isn't serving that purpose if it's so broad that anything can potentially go into the unit. A broad question also presents the danger of reductionism: A changing biome might share some features with a changing society, but they're not the same.

One way to deal with a too-broad essential question is to discuss why the theme is important for students to consider, and write a more specific question that suggests the important ideas. Since the teachers are drawn to the theme of change because their fifth-graders' lives are changing, they could use the question, *How does one change lead to more changes?* or *What are the best ways to respond to change?* Other questions about change that would have more unit-focusing potential than *How do things change?* could be *How do we know if a change is for the better?* or *How can we predict the outcome of a change?* or *What makes people want to change?*

If an essential question is too broad because it contains a general or vague term, like "change," another way to revise it is to choose a more specific term. Depending on the valued focus, the fifth-grade teachers can use a term like "ripple effect" or "adaptation" in their question. Students are also more likely to notice a more specific term like "adaptation" when it appears in different classes than a more general term like "change."

A third way to deal with a broad question is to use it in a gradewide strand. You might imagine the fifth-grade teachers referring to the *How do things change?* question whenever it's relevant throughout the year. Since strands aren't as organized and time-bound as units, it becomes even more important to refer to them explicitly, both with your students so they recognize it when it appears, and with your colleagues so you can refer to each others' examples with your own students and help them understand meaningful similarities and differences between how the topic manifests in different classes.

TWO KINDS OF CROSS-DISCIPLINARY UNITS

A unit, again, is a time-bound study of a particular topic. Many cross-disciplinary units are time-bound in that the students study a concept simultaneously in different classes. Perhaps for several weeks in October, sixth graders learn about immigration in history class while in English they're reading Shaun Tan's *The Arrival*, a graphic novel about a man's experience coming to a new place. Though students might be more likely to connect ideas that are presented at around the same time, those who enjoy learning different things in different classes (or who don't happen to be jazzed about immigration) are just waiting for October to end.

An alternative to the concurrent cross-disciplinary unit is a unit that "rolls" from one class to another (Porosoff 2013). A rolling unit begins in one class, looking like a regular old discipline-based unit in that subject. Over time, though, the unit appears in a second class, and perhaps even a third and a fourth. A diagram showing how a unit can "roll" from class to class is in figure 9.1.

Instead of thinking about a concept in different classes simultaneously, students examine it in one class at a time, incorporating knowledge and skills they learn to help them move forward into something more advanced—like how a snowball rolling down a hill gathers in size and momentum. Students are more likely to understand a larger concept if they can develop that understanding over time. They're also less likely to get bored if they're not bombarded with a topic in every class at once.

ORGANIZING A MULTI-CLASS UNIT

Crossing disciplines is usually easier in schools where one teacher is responsible for several subjects. A unit that spans multiple classes is necessarily more complicated. Involving multiple people means you'll be able to share the work of unit design, and it might even be fun! Even if you struggle and argue as you write values-congruent lessons and an assessment task, the act of working together on something you all value will probably end up being a healthy team-building exercise. Here are some

How does our setting affect our potential to be successful? What can we do to become more successful within our setting?

Course/Time	Unit	Relevant Content	Assessment
Science (February)	**Evolution:** *How does setting affect the success of organisms?*	Different traits within a species are coded in DNA; new variations occur because of mutations. Members of a species must compete for resources to survive. Variations make some individuals better adapted to their environment and more likely to survive, reproduce, and pass helpful traits to their offspring. Over time, helpful variations may accumulate in a species while unhelpful traits may disappear.	Make a cartoon showing how a species adapts to environmental pressures. Include examples of trait variation, competition for resources, environmental conditions for which some individuals are genetically better adapted, and selection for helpful traits.
History (March)	**Mesopotamia:** *How does setting affect the success of a civilization and the people within it?*	Plant domestication and the rise of agriculture led to a sedentary instead of a nomadic hunter-gatherer lifestyle. Settlements led to the concept of private property and required a more organized system of government. Settled life also led to economic specialization, since not everyone had to look for or grow food. Organized government and economic specialization led to social stratification: rulers, priests, merchants, scientists, farmers, and slaves.	Create a travel brochure about Mesopotamian society that includes the concepts of sedentary life, organized government, economic specialization, and social stratification.
English (April)	**Success on Mango Street:** *Who gets access to success in their setting? How can people get more access to success in their settings?*	In *The House on Mango Street*, access to success is related to race, class, and gender. The main character, Esperanza, at first just wants to leave Mango Street but then begins thinking of ways to change her setting so others have increased access to success. "Success" can mean financial gain, social status, inclusion in a group, adaptability, self-actualization, etc. People have access to different types of success in different settings.	Using The House on Mango Street as a model, write a series of vignettes showing ways you're succeeding within your setting and ways your setting limits your ability to succeed.
Math (May)	**Functions and Graphing:** *How can I use algebra to show how my successes relate to my setting and to help me gain access to success?*	Solving problems involving rates and unit rates, finding a percent of increase or decrease, determining whether a relation is a function, graphing functions, choosing data to collect and graph, and interpreting the graphs can help people set goals.	Write, graph, and explain a series of equations that show (1) how successful you are in different areas of your life and (2) what factors affect these successes. Present goals for how you will maintain or change your behaviors and setting to ensure greater success rates in

tips to help you make a multi-class unit and the process of planning it go more smoothly.

Begin with a Shared Experience

A unit that takes place in multiple classes still needs a single beginning. Providing a shared beginning experience for the whole grade—such as a speaker, text, performance, field trip, or community service project—allows different classes to refer back to this common experience as the unit goes forward. In rolling units, the students' experiences in one class form the foundation for learning in another class.

Create a Multi-Class Project

A multi-class unit gives students more opportunities to work with new ideas and skills, but not necessarily more *meaningful* opportunities to do so. A multi-class project creates a meaningful context for students to do the work of the unit and becomes a concrete manifestation of their growing understandings. For example, students could do a project on children's health where they collect data in science, analyze it in math, and discuss its relationship to the changing neighborhood in history.

Refer Frequently to the Essential Question

If a unit takes place in multiple classrooms with multiple teachers, the students might not even realize the material is all part of one unit or understand interconnections between lessons unless their teachers make these explicit. You can post the essential question in all the classrooms, put it on all the unit materials, and give students frequent opportunities to work with it in discussions or writing assignments.

Make an Adjustable Unit Calendar

What needs to happen in which classes, and in what order? As with any unit, you'll need to organize the lessons to lead students to the understandings you value. Here, you'll need to work together to make a unit calendar that works for each individual class and for the unit as a whole. Also consider making a student version of the unit calendar for their reference in multiple classes.

Sticking to the calendar helps keep everyone organized and know what's happening in the unit, but what if someone doesn't finish a lesson that's supposed to lead into an activity in another class? What if someone comes up with a new idea that will affect everyone else? What if a student asks a question no one expected? During the unit, a daily check-in (in person or via email) about that day's classes will keep everyone informed of any updates, changes, or new ideas.

MULTI-CLASS ASSESSMENTS

Imagine a history and English unit that uses the question *How does the teller influence the tale?* In history, the students examine the Civil War from various Union and Confederate perspectives and read Paul Fleischman's *Bull Run*, a novel with sixteen narrators who are diverse in terms of location, race, gender, national origin, socioeconomic status, and occupation. In English, the students read Jessica Leader's novel *Nice and Mean* and discuss how its two narrators describe themselves, each other, and their surroundings similarly and differently.

The English and history teachers decide to create a single assessment for their unit. Each student writes a two-narrator story set during the Civil War, with the English teacher evaluating the story's use of characterization and dialogue, and the history teacher evaluating the accuracy of its historical images and perspectives.

A task that spans multiple disciplines and classes will be complex, so the students will likely need more support, but they'll also benefit from the challenge. Using one assessment for multiple subjects allows students to consolidate their understandings and put time into producing one excellent piece of work. If the assessment spans multiple classes, the students will also get the advantage of feedback from multiple teachers and multiple sets of classmates, as long as the teachers set aside class time for their students to do the work, get the help, and develop the understandings they'll need.

It's hard even in one class to make sure you're teaching all the skills students need to do well on an assessment—especially skills associated with the task but not your discipline. A math teacher might not assign a video project just for his class because teaching kids how to use cameras and editing software would take too much time away from solving equations, but he might be willing to teach *some* videography skills if his colleagues pick up the rest in their classes. In a multi-class unit, there are more potential experts who can teach skills like these, and no one teacher needs to devote as much class time to them.

On the other hand, the diffused responsibility for teaching skills that don't relate to anyone's subject means it's possible *no one* will teach them, and the whole team might end up frustrated or even blaming each other when the students' work is sub par. As a team, you'll need to decide who teaches what and how to allocate class time fairly.

You'll also need to decide on how you'll evaluate the students' work. You might come up with separate grades on your own or one grade together. You might work as a team to write assignment guidelines, or you might each contribute separate criteria to a single rubric. There isn't a "right" way; you and your colleagues will need to come up with one that works for your shared purposes.

Using one assessment for multiple classes presupposes that your team will be able to find a task that serves everyone's values. If you don't, then each teacher can just write a separate assessment task for his or her class.

GETTING COLLEAGUES INTERESTED

Liz's sixth-grade science classes do an intensive study of freshwater biomes, beginning with a field trip to a lake. While chaperoning this trip, the social studies teacher Ariana learns that the fisheries in the lake have been depleted over the years. On the bus back, Ariana and Liz talk about a possible integrated unit. The kids learn about the ecological factors leading to the depleted fisheries in science class in October. In social studies, their November unit is on government, to coincide with elections, and they learn about how laws get made. Ariana and Liz want to have the sixth graders write letters to their local legislature asking for protections for the fish.

As Liz and Ariana get more excited about their unit, they start talking about how other colleagues could get involved, too. "In music, Brandon could have them write songs to raise awareness about the fisheries," Liz says. "Ooh—and in math, Javaid could help them figure out percentages of fish stocks that have been depleted over the last thirty years."

Curriculum planning can move quickly from values to goals—units, projects, and lessons. Excitement about a goal can be contagious, but it can also be alienating to colleagues who didn't participate in creating the goal. Not everyone in a group will share the same values, prioritize their values in the same way, or want to serve those values with the same goal. Brandon might want his students to appreciate music as music, and not as a means of persuasion. Even if Javaid is an environmental activist and feels thrilled that his students are doing the fish unit in other classes, a study of percentages might not fit into his existing math curriculum.

Instead of trying to convince others to "buy in" to your goals, try talking about the values it serves. Liz and Ariana want their students to understand connections between themselves and their surroundings and to take action in the community. If they hope more teachers on their team will join in the fishery fun, Liz and Ariana could begin by talking about the values that inspired them to want to do this project and how the project will move them toward these values. Then, they can invite their colleagues to participate in the unit—and might be surprised by creative ways their colleagues think to connect in.

If no one else is interested, then Liz and Ariana can still proceed on their own while continuing to report back to their colleagues about their progress and solicit their help in solving problems that inevitably arise. Eventually, Brandon and Javaid might want to be part of the unit; or they might not, but at least they won't feel shut out.

OVERCOMING LOGISTICAL BARRIERS

Lily teaches drama in grades 9–12. When she tells her ninth graders about their final project, performing one-act plays, she learns that they'll be writing one-act plays in English class that spring. Lily meets with the English 9 teacher, Sunil, who says the students write plays after reading *Six Degrees of Separation* but don't perform them because that would take too much time away from reading and writing. Both teachers like the idea of having their students performing their original one-act plays in drama class. Together, they write an essential question: *How do playwrights and actors both contribute to the meaning of a play?*

As they discuss logistics, Lily realizes that because performing arts are on a rotating schedule where she sees a third of the students each trimester, only the kids who see her in the spring term would be able to use their one-act plays in her class. Sunil thinks it would feel too unfair to his students if only those who happened to take drama in the spring got to perform their work, while those who took music or dance wouldn't. Lily and Sunil are pretty sure they'll have to drop the whole idea.

At schools that prioritize discipline-based classes in the schedule (not to mention in the budget), crossing disciplines can present all kinds of logistical constraints. You can write proposals requesting the time, space, or funding to pursue new initiatives, but these will require administrative approval.

Another way to deal with logistical problems is to bring in more people who have different perspectives to think with you. Could Sunil could move the play-writing unit to the fall so that eventually, all the kids will be able to perform their plays in drama class? Since Lily teaches tenth grade too, could the students write plays as ninth graders with Sunil and then perform them as tenth graders with Lily? Could the music and dance teachers think of ways to incorporate the one-act plays into their classes?

Maybe you're thinking of other ideas—and that's the point. Some logistical barriers will be insurmountable, but often there's a creative solution. The more people you bring in to think about a cross-disciplinary unit, the more likely you are to find a way to make some version of it work. You might even discover that these other people want to get involved.

GOING FOR IT

Interconnections between disciplines don't have to be big to be effective. Try starting with one lesson, or a field trip with valued content from multiple disciplines. These smaller connections might spark ideas for bigger ones. If they involve multiple classes, they'll also give you occasions to talk to your colleagues about your values and see where they overlap. Communication and shared values are necessary ingredients for sustaining a multi-class unit in the long term.

Connecting disciplines even in small ways requires time—to talk, plan, and learn new material that might be way outside your zone of expertise—and even then, the outcome will probably be far from perfect the first year (and even the second and third). But the biggest barriers to creating cross-disciplinary units are usually the internal ones teachers face. *It's too hard. There's too much to think about. I don't know where to begin. It's not going to work. Let's just wait. My course is fine. The students are happy. Let's not rock the boat. It wasn't that great of an idea anyway.*

Yes, cross-disciplinary units involve more disciplines and often more people, and they're almost always harder to design. The good news is that the burden can be shared. Even those third grade teachers working on the Olympics unit have one crucial asset: a willingness to collaborate. If they could come together around a topic, perhaps they could come together again to evaluate the unit and make future units more meaningful.

Coming together to struggle with the challenges of creating something meaningful can strengthen the relationships within your team. As a team, you can decide that crossing disciplines is too complicated and not worth the effort, or you can help each other overcome internal barriers and hold each other accountable—not to a set of standards created by people you've never met or to an administrative initiative, but to your values as teachers.

Increasing Values Congruence over Time

How do we know if our units truly serve our values?

The psychologist Steven Hayes (2005) explains that a value is not a destination but a direction—one you can move in every day. Every day, you have opportunities to teach toward your values. If it's important to you to help students see themselves in the curriculum, you can do that every day. The ongoing nature of values also means you're never finished teaching by them. You helped students see themselves in the curriculum yesterday, so today they can find their work in your class irrelevant? Values don't work that way.

Across a unit, course, or program, you might balance the ways you serve different values—say, helping students see themselves in the curriculum *and also* exposing them to unfamiliar experiences and issues—but you'll always be working to maintain that balance. There is no curricular nirvana. Values-congruent curriculum design is a continual process, and often a challenging and convoluted one.

THE EVOLUTION OF A VALUES-CONGRUENT UNIT

When Allison first started teaching *Of Mice and Men*, the unit was a heap of literary devices and themes. The assessment was an essay where the main goal was to write an introduction that led the reader to a thesis, three body paragraphs that supported the thesis, and a conclusion that summarized the thesis: the dreaded five-paragraph formula. Even though Allison's students could choose to write about any theme or literary device in the book, the assignment wasn't interesting, and neither were the essays it spawned.

After two years of teaching this way, Allison knew she had to change *something*. She valued choice and had done author studies before, so she thought she'd try converting the *Of Mice and Men* unit into an author study where the students could choose *Of Mice and Men*, *The Red Pony*, or *Cannery Row*. Their essential question was, *What makes Steinbeck Steinbeck?* The question gave Allison's seventh graders a purpose for exploring Steinbeck's devices and themes: They were out to discover which ones defined his style. The students enjoyed debating whether a device or theme was "Stein-becky" and sharing examples from their books.

When they were finished reading, the students formed groups where each person had read a different book, and each group worked together to come up with a thesis like "Steinbeck gets his readers to question their first impressions by including characters who seem scary but are actually kind," or "What makes Steinbeck Steinbeck is his use of setting description to foreshadow events." The groups wrote essays together; each student contributed a body paragraph supporting the thesis with examples from his or her book, and the group jointly wrote an introduction about Steinbeck and a conclusion about his style.

Allison was pleased to be teaching the required content and skills in a way that was more consistent with her values of student engagement and choice, deep and purposeful inquiry, and collaboration. Still, the unit wasn't sitting quite right with her. The five-paragraph essays were better but still sounded formulaic. Allison wanted the essays to be "unGoogleable"—work no one else could or would have created. She also wanted her students to write in real-world genres, as opposed to writing one academic essay after another.

That year, the writer David Sobel came to Allison's school to talk about place-based education. At around the same time, the seventh-grade teachers began to look for cross-disciplinary connections. One theme they noticed across science, language, and history was how environment shapes the interactions of anything or anyone living in it. The concept of place was becoming an important cross-disciplinary strand, and Allison wanted it in the English 7 curriculum. In researching Steinbeck for the author study, she'd seen articles about his regionalism—his sense of place.

The unit's new essential questions were *How do writers create a sense of place?* and *How do different people experience the same place differently?* The class studied how Steinbeck's imagery conveys a sense of place and analyzed how characters' experiences of a place depend on access to power, as related to race, gender, and ability. They examined the same literary devices and themes as before, but related them to place. Since the students could have richer conversations about place if they were reading about the *same* place, and since other units now gave students a choice of text, Allison went back to everyone reading *Of Mice and Men*.

The bigger change was the assessment. Instead of writing five-paragraph analyses of Steinbeck, the students showed they understood how writers create a sense of place by doing it themselves, in essays about their neighborhoods. They still learned to write a thesis and gather evidence, but now they were using these skills in personal, authentic, and just plain better writing. The best essays were quirky, like the one about an oddly painted fire hydrant that attracts tourists' attention but that Manhattan locals ignore, or beautifully descriptive, like the one about the white peacock living at Saint John the Divine.

Still, many essays simply asserted that something in the neighborhood was "good" or "unique." ("Sal's makes the best pizza in the world!") Allison wanted her students to make more of a point—not only because a thesis is supposed to be arguable, but because she wanted them all to learn they had important points to make. She also had trouble saying how essays about pizza and peacocks connected to the key themes in *Of Mice and Men*.

That fall, she went to a workshop at Bard College's Institute for Writing and Thinking, where she learned to do a conceptual inquiry using essays, poems, paintings, stories, and other texts. She was so inspired that she decided to put *Of Mice and Men* into conversation with other texts. Since many of Steinbeck's books question societal definitions of success and attempt to redefine success as economic self-sufficiency and social companionship, she wrote the essential questions *What does it mean to be successful?* and *Who gets to be successful?* Allison started looking through her files for texts that might complicate this inquiry.

The class now began the unit by uncovering and challenging their own definitions of success. Next, they analyzed *Of Mice and Men* passages that suggested the author's and characters' ideas of success. Later, they looked at data from the National Agricultural Workers' Survey, Fritjof Capra's essay "Speaking Nature's Language" about the principles of ecosystems, and a video about Landfill Harmonic, a classical music program that uses instruments made from trash. Her class discussed how each text conceptualized success and whether *Of Mice and Men* characters have access to these different kinds of success.

At the end of the unit, the assignment was, "Write an essay exploring your own relationship to someone or something in your neighborhood that you consider successful." The students compiled definitions of success from the unit and then listed things in their neighborhoods—people, groups, natural features, structures, processes, events—that fit those different definitions of "successful."

As they articulated how each thing was successful, the students ended up with many potential thesis statements. They generated images, stories, and even fantasies about their chosen topics; Allison wanted her students to understand how their own experiences and imaginings could be "evidence" in an essay. Their conclusions reviewed how "success" could be defined in different ways and how not everyone has access to the same kinds of success.

Allison's students had connected ideas across multiple and seemingly unrelated texts, drawn on their own experiences, questioned their assumptions, learned transferrable skills, and sounded like themselves in authentic writing that mattered to them. She was happy. After so much work and so many different versions of this unit, was she finally done? Maybe! Table 10.1 charts the evolution of this unit.

The history of Allison's Steinbeck unit shows not a failure to teach by her values but a progression toward them. When she first started teaching the unit, it wasn't "bad," but it didn't lead her students to the meaningful learning that mattered to her.

Table 10.1. Evolution of a Values-Congruent Unit

Unit Title	Of Mice and Men	John Steinbeck Author Study	Portraying a Place	Imagining Success
Essential Questions	None	*What makes Steinbeck Steinbeck?*	*How do writers create a sense of place?* *How do different people experience the same place differently?*	*What does it mean to be successful?* *Who gets to be successful?*
Content	Literary devices: • Imagery • Motifs • Foreshadowing • Symbols • Irony Themes: • Power as related to race, class, gender, ability • Friendship • Loneliness and isolation • Being judged on appearances	An author's style involves using particular devices and themes across different texts. Steinbeck's literary devices: • Imagery • Motifs • Foreshadowing • Symbols • Irony Steinbeck's themes: • Power as related to race, class, gender, ability • Friendship • Loneliness and isolation • Being judged on appearances	Steinbeck creates a strong sense of place using: • Imagery • Motifs • Foreshadowing • Symbols • Irony Each Steinbeck character's experience of the place depends on: • Power as related to race, class, gender, ability • Friendship • Loneliness and isolation • Being judged on appearances	Different ideas about success are embedded in different texts. Success can be: • Economic self-sufficiency • Social companionship • Achieving power in a hierarchy • Freedom • Having one's needs met • Making something valuable out of something worthless • Living in harmony with one's surroundings Access to success in an unjust society can relate to race, class, gender, and ability.

Assessment	Analytical essay Write a formal essay about how Steinbeck uses any literary device or theme in *Of Mice and Men*.	Group analytical essay As a group, write an essay explaining how a particular device or theme defines Steinbeck's writing across his books.	Neighborhood essay Write an essay that creates a strong sense of your neighborhood from your personal perspective.	Neighborhood essay Write an essay exploring your relationship to someone or something in your neighborhood that you consider successful.
Skills	Writing a thesis statement Generating evidence by collecting quotations Writing an introduction that leads the reader to the thesis Writing body paragraphs that include textual evidence Writing a conclusion that summarizes and shows importance	Writing a thesis statement Generating evidence by collecting quotations Writing an introduction that leads the reader to the thesis Writing body paragraphs that include textual evidence Writing a conclusion that summarizes and shows importance	Writing a thesis statement Generating evidence by collecting images from one's personal experience Organizing an essay based on the thesis	Writing a thesis statement Generating evidence by collecting images from one's personal experience and imagination Organizing an essay based on the thesis
Texts	Steinbeck, *Of Mice and Men*	Steinbeck, *Of Mice and Men* Steinbeck, *Cannery Row* Steinbeck, *The Red Pony*	Steinbeck, *Of Mice and Men*	Steinbeck, *Of Mice and Men* National Agricultural Workers Survey data Borondo, street art Townsley et al., Landfill Harmonic movie trailer Chang, "Weed It and Reap" Capra, "Speaking Nature's Language"

Over time, as you struggle to find ways to revise your units, they might become increasingly values-congruent, but the process of designing a values-congruent unit has no endpoint.

UNINTENDED CONSEQUENCES

For one thing, your new unit will create new challenges you didn't expect. Due to the complex interdependent relationships within a system (your school), a small change to one part (your unit) will have ripple effects. Students who learn in math to analyze the distribution of fresh produce in the Bronx might wonder in history about the distribution of resources in ancient Egypt. Students who do service learning by writing Spanish-language pamphlets about preparing for emergencies might need to say things like, "You should buy enough water to last for three days," and now they need lessons on the subjunctive.

Unintended consequences can also surface when you try out a new approach because some aspect of an assignment matches your values, but the resulting work doesn't match other important values. That's what happened to Allison when she first assigned the neighborhood essays during her Steinbeck unit: She valued personal writing, but she also valued depth, and some students' essays were fluffy.

If you try a new approach that doesn't end up serving your values, what do you do? Tweak the unit so your values are better served? Try an entirely different approach? Revert back to what you did before? If you voluntarily tried something new, it probably means that at least one of your values wasn't being served, so going back to the old way might not be your best choice.

SHIFTING PRIORITIES

Even if you anticipate every effect of your new unit, you'll still need to keep working on it because you'll do an incomplete job aligning it to your values. A unit of study is always a compromise between multiple values within the confines of time. Some math teachers say they value giving real-life problems but that they also value teaching skills for mastery, and they don't have time to do both as well as they'd like. Art teachers who value teaching process might wonder if their students create enough products or feel that the products aren't of high enough quality.

You might be unhappy with the way you prioritize your values one year and take corrective action the next year. What values do you feel like are in conflict with each other? How do you resolve those conflicts? Does your solution still sit right with you the following year?

CHANGING TIMES

Even if you anticipate every outcome and you find the perfect balance between your values, you're still never done designing values-congruent curriculum. Your students will always be different, asking new questions and throwing you new challenges. If you're lucky, your colleagues will share ideas that perturb and inspire you. Articles and workshops will push against the ways you're teaching or give you new insights you'll want to act on. Even events in your personal life, videos you watch, things you notice on walks and in conversations—they'll all come back to haunt your perfectly-aligned units.

The world you're teaching about is also changing. Heidi Hayes Jacobs (2010) borrows the term "upgrading" from the information technology field to describe how teachers make their curriculum more relevant for our times by replacing dated assessment practices (like oral reports) with more contemporary ones (like TED talks), embedding media and cultural literacy skills, and rethinking content in light of our rapidly changing world. Every day, scientists make discoveries, history unfolds right on TV, and artists make new work. The world's knowledge base and problems are growing exponentially. How can your units remain the same?

Values-congruent curriculum design is a lifelong (or at least career-long) process, and even if you're the most meticulous and determined teacher in the world, you'll never get your unit exactly perfect. Something in the system will change: other units, your colleagues, your students, the standards, the technology—something. And you'll change too. What do you do when after all the work you've done on a unit, there's still a values congruence issue?

ACTION RESEARCH

James McKernan (2008) imagines "a curriculum conceived not as a final and prescriptive solution, but as a set of hypotheses" (115), and that the people best positioned to test these "hypotheses" aren't outside researchers but teachers. You have the professional judgment to interrogate the curriculum and the capacity to change it. You can study how well your curriculum "works"—the extent to which its results match your shifting personal and institutional values. This process of asking questions about your own practice, collecting and analyzing your own data, and using that data to make decisions is called action research. Imagine that while reading her students' neighborhood essays, Allison begins to suspect that the girls are getting better grades than the boys, which upsets her because she greatly values acting fairly and creating an environment where all her students can excel. She takes an average of the girls' grades and an average of the boys', and she discovers that indeed, the girls' average is significantly higher.

Much more difficult than collecting and analyzing the data is explaining it. Allison begins to question everything about her unit and teaching practices. *Am I just sexist? Do I hand higher grades to girls because I like them better or—ugh—because I think their self-esteems can't handle lower ones? Is there something about analyzing one's connection to a neighborhood success story that appeals more to the average girl than the average boy? Am I inadvertently giving girls more feedback that results in their better performance?*

Even if Allison doesn't figure out why the grade discrepancy occurred, she isn't powerless to make her curriculum more values-congruent in the future. She decides to keep collecting assessment data to see whether the gender discrepancies continue throughout her course and in future years or if it's specific to this unit and group. She asks her students—male and female—about their experiences in her class to look for differences in their perceptions. She even starts setting a timer while conferencing with students to make sure she's giving each one a fair share of her time and feedback, and she tries to account for any biases as she's grading. She keeps thinking about how to design gender-fair curriculum.

What's empowering about action research is that you don't need money or special resources to do it. All you need is a willingness to examine your curriculum and potentially change it to make it more values congruent. Like most processes that lead to school change, action research works even better if you can do it in a group. If you're interested in learning more about action research, Richard Sagor's *The Action Research Guidebook* describes what it is and how to do it in a classroom setting.

CRITICAL FRIENDS GROUPS

Designing values-congruent curriculum can be a constant uphill battle, and it helps to have supportive colleagues who are excited to talk through your units with you, push back when you make self-limiting statements, and provoke you with their insights. Supportive colleagues will also help you hold yourself accountable to your goals.

Try finding a few colleagues who'd be willing to meet regularly (in person or in an online forum) to review assignments, student work, or curriculum maps to see if they match your values. You'll also learn a lot from looking at *their* work products and hearing their dilemmas. If you want to formalize the work you're doing with supportive colleagues, you might consider establishing a critical friends group (CFG), which is simply a group of educators who work together with the goal of all members making their own teaching more values congruent.

The School Reform Initiative has a fantastic website with information about how to conduct a CFG. On the website are two protocols that are particularly helpful for teachers who want to determine the extent to which their units are values congruent and what to do next.

The first is the Collaborative Assessment Conference Protocol (Seidel). Use this to look closely at a piece of student work. In the protocol, you show a piece of student work: a math problem set, a sculpture, a weightlifting log, or whatever makes sense for your class. You give no background about the work; you simply show it to your colleagues, who describe and ask questions about the work without judging it. Later, you can respond to whichever questions interest you and give whatever background you choose to give about the assignment and the student.

You might find yourself amazed by what the group notices that the presenter didn't, and by the fact that just observations and questions illuminate the ways the student's work does and doesn't match the presenter's values. This protocol helpfully keeps colleagues' judgments out of the conversation; the focus is on values.

Another very helpful School Reform Initiative tool is called the Tuning Protocol (McDonald and Allen). Use this to look at your own work: your assignment, materials, rubric, syllabus, or map for a particular unit. For this protocol, you bring a specific question for the group—a question about how your work could better match up with a particular value.

A science teacher who values student curiosity and who notices her students aren't showing all that much curiosity when doing a recent lab on pH, could present the lab assignment (and perhaps materials from lessons leading up to the lab) and ask "How can I foster my students' curiosity about pH through a lab activity?" A history teacher who values thoroughness, and notices some students gave very cursory explanations of unfair labor practices on a recent test (even though he'd so thoroughly gone over the issues in class!), could ask something like, "How can I make sure students give more thorough explanations?"

During the protocol, you first explain the relevant parts of your curriculum and then ask the group your question. The group asks questions to get more information, examines your work to see if it's "in tune" with your valued goal, and then gives feedback on how the curriculum you're presenting is already values congruent and where you could modify it so the results will be more in tune with your values.

You might leave these sessions surprised by your own successes, impressed by your colleagues' insights into your work, and ready to revise your unit. It can also be an immensely powerful experience to have colleagues see your work and recognize the things you value in it.

VALUES-CONGRUENT PROFESSIONAL DEVELOPMENT

Some of the ways Allison revised her Steinbeck unit seem to have arisen by pure chance: David Sobel just happened to be speaking at her school about the concept of place, giving her the idea to rebuild the unit around that concept, and later she just happened be at the Bard workshop, where she realized she could design the unit using a multi-text inquiry format.

As magically serendipitous as those moments of inspiration might have felt at the time, they were really just the result of her engaging in professional development that matched her values as a teacher. Educating for sustainability, using local knowledge, and fostering the students' ability to create their own ideas are all values she holds deeply, so she attended Sobel's roundtable and Bard's workshop to serve those values.

If you see a professional development opportunity—a book, lecture, workshop, or conference, or something within your school like a peer observation or roundtable—it's less important that the topic matches your curriculum than that the underlying values match your own. As long as you go into the experience with openness and curiosity, a connection to your curriculum will present itself eventually (and sometimes immediately).

SETTING GOALS

Values aren't goals you can check off a to-do list, but you can set goals in the service of your values. Hayes (2005) uses a hiking metaphor to show both the difference between goals and values and how you can set goals in the service of values: If living by your values is like hiking east, setting a goal is like looking east, finding a big tree, and hiking toward it. "East" is abstract, but a big tree is a concrete marker, and if you get to the tree, you know you've gone east.

You might have heard of "SMART" goals before. This version (adapted for educators from Russ Harris 2009, 210) incorporates values. Here, a "SMART" goal is:

Specific

What exactly will you do? When? Where? How? Who else is involved? What resources do you need?

An example of a vague goal is, "I'm going to make sure my units are aligned," or, "I will have my students write more." These goals don't help you visualize a particular outcome or what you'll need to do to get there.

A specific goal would be, "I will make one assessment each trimester a writing project," or "I will ask my students to write an explanation for the challenge problem every week," or even "I will speak to my colleagues in the humanities to brainstorm ideas for how I can use writing in my math class." These goals create concrete images. When you can visualize a goal in your mind, you can also see it when it's happening in real life and know you've successfully achieved it.

Which aspect of your curriculum will become the focus of your attention. Will you work on a particular unit? Some element of your course or program?

Meaningful

The goal genuinely comes from your values. You aren't following a rule, trying to please a colleague or administrator, living up to a particular self-image, or avoiding a negative feeling like anxiety or disappointment. You might focus on values that feel important right now and that you're not living by as much as you'd like to be in your work as an educator.

What values will you be serving as you work on this part of your curriculum?

Active

The goal is something you'd have an easier time doing awake than asleep. An example of a "sleeper's goal" would be, "I won't give as many worksheets." It's easier to avoid giving worksheets if you're asleep! An active goal would be, "For the water cycle unit, I'll replace the activity packet with a model-building project."

An active goal is important because sometimes teachers decide to stop using a practice they've relied on for years without a clear plan for how to get the same benefits. An English teacher who values teaching transferable skills and has seen evidence that grammar taught through skill drills doesn't transfer to the students' writing decides to stop giving grammar drills. Great, but how are his students learning grammar now? In trying to serve his value of transfer, he's now neglecting other values! An active goal means you're *doing* something in the service of values you've neglected in the past.

Realistic

The goal is achievable within the context of your current school's schedule, facilities, and budget. There might be external barriers, but there's also some possibility that you'll find creative ways around or through them.

You can make your goal more realistic by finding sources of support. These can include books, workshops, observations, and formal or informal critical friends groups to help you develop and refine your curriculum. Use your colleagues as well as your school's learning specialists, nurse, psychologist, technology integrators, librarians, cafeteria staff, parents, and anyone else as consultants and mentors.

Time-Limited

The goal has a reasonable due date. It's not a "someday" goal. You might consider setting a series of goals over increasingly longer time frames: a small goal you can achieve today, a larger goal you can achieve this month, and even larger goals you can achieve this year. Your smaller goals might be precursors to the bigger ones—like attending a workshop on teaching content through drama next month and redesigning a unit to incorporate a drama-based assessment next year—or you might have several very different goals that only relate to each other in that they all serve your values.

On the due date of your goal, check in with a supportive colleague. If you accomplished your goal, talk about how, and if you didn't, talk about what got in the way. The point isn't to get bogged down in guilt if you weren't successful or even in pride if you were. The point is to set new goals and get help overcoming internal barriers to achieving them.

THE TEACHER YOU WANT TO BE

Allison's original Steinbeck unit wasn't bad, but the teacher *she* wanted to be was someone who helped students make classic texts relevant to their lives, explore questions of identity and social justice, and become more critical and creative readers, writers, and thinkers. Way back in chapter 1, you met Henry, whose dinosaur unit was perfectly respectable before he went to the mural workshop, but the teacher *he* wanted to be was someone who gave his students opportunities to work together, use their imaginations, and remember the content.

Allison and Henry can't tell the stories of their other units with the same kind of triumph they feel when they talk about Steinbeck and dinosaur murals, because they still aren't the teachers they want to be when it comes to the rest of their courses. It's not that they can't think of new ideas for their other units; they've tried lots of approaches and so far, they haven't found ones that the teachers they want to be would use. They're also struggling with the fact that their units don't add up to a coherent course. But they're setting new goals every year, with their values to guide them.

Back in the 1980s, there was a commercial for milk where a girl complained about her appearance to her increasingly older self in the mirror. The older girl encouraged her younger self by showing her how beautiful her skin, hair, and body would eventually look (with a little help from milk, of course). If you can get past this commercial's questionable message that girls can be happy only if they're pretty, you might like idea of envisioning the person you'll ultimately become and imagining the encouraging words that person might say to you as you struggle along.

If you imagine the teacher you want to be, what does he or she do? What does this teacher's classroom look like? What are the students doing? If this teacher you want to be could speak to you, what encouraging words could he or she offer?

This work is hard. You're willing to do it anyway. Best wishes to you as you design values-congruent curriculum and become the teacher you want to be.

Bibliography

Alexie, Sherman, and Ellen Forney. *The Absolutely True Diary of a Part-Time Indian*. New York: Little, Brown, 2007.

Banks, James A. *Educating Citizens in a Multicultural Society*. New York: Teachers College, 1997.

Barkley, Elizabeth F., K. Patricia Cross, and Claire Howell Major. *Collaborative Learning Techniques: A Handbook for College Faculty*. San Francisco: Jossey-Bass, 2005.

Biglan, Anthony, and Steven C. Hayes. "Should the Behavioral Sciences Become More Pragmatic? The Case for Functional Contextualism in Research on Human Behavior." *Applied and Preventive Psychology* 5.1 (1996): 47–57.

Brophy, Jere, and Janet Alleman. "A Caveat: Curriculum Integration Isn't Always a Good Idea." *Educational Leadership* 42.2 (1991): 66.

Capra, Fritjof. "Speaking Nature's Language: Principles for Sustainability." In *Ecological Literacy: Educating Our Children for a Sustainable World*, edited by Michael K. Stone and Zenobia Barlow, 18–29. San Francisco: Sierra Club, 2005.

Chang, T. Susan. "Weed It And Reap: A Meal With Nature's Outcasts." *NPR*. NPR, 23 June 2010. Web. 15 May 2014.

Ciarrochi, Joseph, Louise Hayes, and Ann Bailey. *Get Out of Your Mind and into Your Life for Teens: A Guide to Living an Extraordinary Life*. Oakland, CA: Instant Help, 2012.

Cirillo, Jennifer, and Emily Hoyler, eds. "Linking the Big Ideas of Sustainability with Essential Questions." *The Guide to Education for Sustainability* 2011: 36–37. *Sustainable Schools Project*. Shelburne Farms. www.sustainableschoolsproject.org/file/371/EFSGuide2011.pdf.

Cisneros, Sandra. *The House on Mango Street*. New York: Vintage, 1991.

Csikszentmihalyi, Mihaly. *Finding Flow: The Psychology of Engagement with Everyday Life*. New York: Basic, 1997.

Darling-Hammond, Linda. *The Flat World and Education: How America's Commitment to Equity Will Determine Our Future*. New York: Teachers College, 2010.

"Drover (Australian)." *Wikipedia: The Free Encyclopedia*. Wikimedia Foundation, Inc. 14 Mar. 2013. Web. 11 July 2013. http://en.wikipedia.org/wiki/Drover_(Australian).

Essential Atlas of Ecology. Hauppauge, NY: Barron's Educational Series, 2005.

Fleischman, Paul, and David Frampton. *Bull Run*. New York: HarperCollins, 1993.

Fox, Eric. "Constructing a Pragmatic Science of Learning and Instruction with Functional Contextualism." *Educational Technology Research and Development* 54.1 (2006): 5–36.

Freire, Paulo. *Pedagogy of the Oppressed*. New York: Continuum, 2000.

Geist, Eugene. "The Anti-Anxiety Curriculum: Combating Math Anxiety in the Classroom." *Journal of Instructional Psychology* 37.1 (2010): 24–31.

Gonick, Larry, and Alice B. Outwater. *The Cartoon Guide to the Environment*. New York: HarperCollins, 1996.

Graham, Steve, and Dolores Perin. "A Meta-analysis of Writing Instruction for Adolescent Students." *Journal of Educational Psychology* 99.3 (2007): 445–76.

Hansberry, Lorraine. *A Raisin in the Sun*. New York: Vintage, 1994.

Harris, Russ. *ACT Made Simple: An Easy-to-Read Primer on Acceptance and Commitment Therapy*. Oakland, CA: New Harbinger Publications, 2009.

———. *The Happiness Trap: How to Stop Struggling and Start Living*. Boston: Trumpeter, 2008.

———. "Values Worksheet." *Worksheets to Use with the Happiness Trap*. 2008b. Web. 4 July 2013. www.thehappinesstrap.com/upimages/Values_Questionnaire.pdf.

Hassard, Jack. "Common Core Values: Do They Include Authoritarianism?" *Education Week Teacher: Living in Dialogue*. Editorial Projects in Education, 8 May 2012. Web. 25 Apr. 2014.

Hayes, Steven C., Linda J. Hayes, and Hayne W. Reese. "Finding the Philosophical Core: A Review of Stephen C. Pepper's World Hypotheses." *Journal of the Experimental Analysis of Behavior* 50.1 (1988): 97–111.

Hayes, Steven C., and Spencer Smith. *Get Out of Your Mind and Into Your Life: The New Acceptance and Commitment Therapy*. Oakland, CA: New Harbinger Publications, 2005.

Himmele, Pérsida, and William Himmele. *Total Participation Techniques: Making Every Student an Active Learner*. Alexandria, VA: ASCD, 2011.

Horton, Tom. *Bay Country: Reflections on the Chesapeake*. New York: Ticknor and Fields, 1989.

Jacobs, Heidi Hayes. "Interdisciplinary Learning in Your Classroom: Implementation." *Interdisciplinary Learning in Your Classroom: Implementation*. Educational Broadcasting Corporation, 2004. Web. 04 June 2013. www.thirteen.org/edonline/concept2class/ interdisciplinary/implementation.html.

———. *Curriculum 21: Essential Education for a Changing World*. Alexandria, VA: Association for Supervision and Curriculum Development, 2010.

Karpicke, Jeffrey D., and Janell R. Blunt. "Retrieval Practice Produces More Learning than Elaborative Studying with Concept Mapping." *Science* 331.6018 (2011): 772–75.

Kliebard, Herbert M. *The Struggle for the American Curriculum, 1893–1958*. 3rd ed. New York: Routledge, 2004.

Krathwohl, David R. "A Revision of Bloom's Taxonomy: An Overview." *Theory into Practice* 41.4 (2002): 212–18.

Landfill Harmonic Movie Teaser. Dir. Graham Townsley. Prod. Rodolfo Madero, Jorge Maldonado, and Monica Barrios. *Vimeo*. Vimeo, LLC, 24 Oct. 2012. Web. 17 June 2013. http://vimeo.com/52129103.

Lasley, Thomas J., Thomas J. Matczynski, and James B. Rowley. *Instructional Models: Strategies for Teaching in a Diverse Society*. Belmont, CA: Wadsworth/Thomson Learning, 2002.

Leader, Jessica. *Nice and Mean*. New York: Simon and Schuster Children's Pub., 2010.

Lyon, George Ella. "Where I'm From." *Where I'm From: Where Poems Come From*. Spring, TX: Absey, 1999. 3.

Martinez, Sylvia Libow, and Gary Stager. *Invent to Learn: Making, Tinkering, and Engineering in the Classroom*. Torrance, CA: Constructing Modern Knowledge, 2013.

McDonald, Joseph, and David Allen. "Tuning Protocol." *School Reform Initiative*. Web. 3 May 2014. http://schoolreforminitiative.org/doc/tuning.pdf.

McDonough, William, and Michael Braungart. *Cradle to Cradle: Remaking the Way We Make Things*. New York: North Point, 2002.

———. *The Upcycle: Beyond Sustainability - Designing for Abundance*. New York: North Point, 2013.

McKernan, James. *Curriculum and Imagination: Process Theory, Pedagogy and Action Research*. London: Routledge, 2008.

McTighe, Jay, and Grant Wiggins. *Essential Questions: Opening Doors to Student Understanding*. Alexandria, VA: Assn for Supervision & Curriculum, 2013.

Meadows, Donella H., and Diana Wright. *Thinking in Systems: A Primer*. White River Junction, VT: Chelsea Green Pub., 2008.

Musselwhite, David. "Values of the Common Core: Equity, Competition, and Collaboration." *Education Week Teacher: Living in Dialogue*. Editorial Projects in Education, 15 May 2012. Web. 25 Apr. 2014.

National Governors Association Center for Best Practices and Council of Chief State School Officers. "Mission Statement." *Common Core State Standards Initiative*. National Governors Association Center for Best Practices, Council of Chief State School Officers, Washington, DC, 2010. Web. 18 May 2013. www.corestandards.org.

———. "Frequently Asked Questions." *Common Core State Standards Initiative*. National Governors Association Center for Best Practices, Council of Chief State School Officers, 2012. Web. 26 June 2013. www.corestandards.org/resources/frequently-asked-questions.

Nieto, Sonia, and Patty Bode. *Affirming Diversity: The Sociopolitical Context of Multicultural Education*. 5th ed. Boston: Pearson/Allyn and Bacon, 2008.

Outwater, Alice B. *Water: A Natural History*. New York: Basic, 1996.

Paschen, Elise, and Dominique Raccah. *Poetry Speaks Who I Am*. Naperville, IL: Jabberwocky, 2010.

Pink, Daniel H. *A Whole New Mind: Why Right-Brainers Will Rule the Future*. New York: Riverhead, 2006.

Porosoff, Lauren. "That's How We Roll: Integrating the Curriculum." *AMLE Magazine* 1.3 (2013): 25–27.

Ravitch, Diane. *The Death and Life of the Great American School System: How Testing and Choice Are Undermining Education*. New York: Basic, 2011.

"Ringmaster (Circus)." *Wikipedia: The Free Encyclopedia*. Wikimedia Foundation, Inc. 9 June 2013. Web. 11 July 2013. http://en.wikipedia.org/wiki/Ringmaster_(circus).

Ritchhart, Ron, Mark Church, and Karin Morrison. *Making Thinking Visible: How to Promote Engagement, Understanding, and Independence for All Learners*. San Francisco, CA: Jossey-Bass, 2011.

Robinson, Ken. "Ken Robinson Says Schools Kill Creativity." *TED: Ideas Worth Spreading*. TED Conferences, LLC, June 2006. Web. 28 May 2013. www.ted.com/talks/ken_robinson_says_schools_kill_creativity.html.

Sagor, Richard. *The Action Research Guidebook: A Four-step Process for Educators and School Teams*. Thousand Oaks, CA: Corwin, 2005.

Satrapi, Marjane. *Persepolis*. New York: Pantheon, 2003.

Schiro, Michael Stephen. "Introduction to the Curriculum Ideologies." *Curriculum Theory: Conflicting Visions and Enduring Concerns*. Thousand Oaks, CA: SAGE Publications, 2013. 1–14.

Seidel, Steve, et al. "Collaborative Assessment Conference Protocol." *School Reform Initiative.* Web. 3 May 2014. http://schoolreforminitiative.org/doc/cac.pdf.

Seligman, Martin E. P. *Authentic Happiness: Using the New Positive Psychology to Realize Your Potential for Lasting Fulfillment.* New York: Free, 2002.

Siedentop, Daryl, Peter A. Hastie, and Der Mars, Hans Van. *Complete Guide to Sport Education.* Champaign, IL: Human Kinetics, 2004.

Slattery, Patrick. *Curriculum Development in the Postmodern Era: Teaching and Learning in an Age of Accountability.* 3rd ed. New York: Routledge, 2013.

Sleeter, Christine E. *Un-standardizing Curriculum: Multicultural Teaching in the Standards-based Classroom.* New York: Teacher College, 2005.

Steinbeck, John. *Of Mice and Men.* New York: Penguin, 1993.

Stroessner, Steven, and Catherine Good. "What Are the Consequences of Stereotype Threat?" *ReducingStereotypeThreat.org.* Consortium of High Achievement and Success and Barnard College, 8 Feb. 2009. Web. 25 Dec. 2013.

Sweeney, Linda Booth. *When a Butterfly Sneezes: A Guide for Helping Kids Explore Interconnections in Our World through Favorite Stories.* Waltham, MA: Pegasus Communications, 2001.

Tan, Shaun. *The Arrival.* New York: Arthur A. Levine, 2007.

Tokuhama-Espinosa, Tracey. *Mind, Brain, and Education Science: A Comprehensive Guide to the New Brain-based Teaching.* New York: W.W. Norton, 2010.

United States Department of Labor, Office of the Assistant Secretary for Policy, and Aguirre International. *Findings from the National Agricultural Workers Survey (NAWS) 2001– 2002: A Demographic and Employment Profile of United States Farm Workers.* By Daniel Carroll, Ruth M. Samardick, Scott Bernard, Susan Gabbard, and Trish Hernandez.

United States Department of Labor, 2005. Research Report No. 9. Web. www.doleta.gov/agworker/report9/naws_rpt9.pdf.

Urban, Wayne J., and Jennings L. Wagoner, Jr. *American Education: A History.* 5th ed. New York: Routledge, 2014.

Vilardi, Teresa, and Mary Chang. *Writing-based Teaching: Essential Practices and Enduring Questions.* Albany: State University of New York, 2009.

Wiggins, Grant P., and Jay McTighe. *Schooling by Design: Mission, Action, and Achievement.* Alexandria, VA: Association for Supervision and Curriculum Development, 2007.

——. *Understanding by Design.* 2nd ed. Alexandria, VA: Association for Supervision and Curriculum Development, 2005.

Willis, Judy. "A Neurologist Makes the Case for the Video Game Model as a Learning Tool." *Edutopia*. The George Lucas Educational Foundation, 14 Apr. 2011. Web. 25 May 2013. www.edutopia.org/blog/video-games-learning-student-engagement-judy-willis.

———. "Three Brain-Based Teaching Strategies to Build Executive Function in Students (Part 4 of 7)." *Edutopia*. The George Lucas Educational Foundation, 5 Oct. 2011. Web. 25 May 2013. www.edutopia.org/blog/brain-based-teaching-strategies-judy-willis.

Wilson, Kelly G., and Troy DuFrene. *Mindfulness for Two: An Acceptance and Commitment Therapy Approach to Mindfulness in Psychotherapy*. Oakland, CA: New Harbinger Publications, 2009.

Wilson, Kelly G., Emily K. Sandoz, Jennifer Kitchens, and Miguel Roberts. "The Valued Living Questionnaire: Defining and Measuring Valued Action within a Behavioral Framework." *The Psychological Record* 60 (2010): 249–72.

Yadavaia, James E., and Steven C. Hayes. "Values in Acceptance and Commitment Therapy: A Comparison with Four Other Approaches." *Hellenic Journal of Psychology* 6 (2009): 244–72.

Yezierska, Anzia, and Alice Kessler-Harris. *Bread Givers: A Novel*. New York: Persea, 2003.

Index

action research, 135–36

aligned curriculum, 69–72, *73*, 119, 135; challenges in achieving, 74, 78–82; examples of, 69–71, *75–77*; resistance to, 71–72; self-assessing for, 82–83

arts, 1–2, 7–9, 27, *30*, 31, 38, 57, 62, *87*, 95, 105, 107, 116, 126, 134

assessments: aligned to the unit, 71–74, 78–82; definition of, 25, 53; for multiple classes, 124; mix of, 88–92, *104*, 107–9; project-based, 45, 67; purposes of, *21–22*, 53–54; student choice in, 59–60; supporting student success in, 60–63; timing of, 60; types of, 54–57; "values-dense," 57–59; writing guidelines for, 63–67

autonomy in curriculum design, 13–14

backward design, 88

barriers to teaching by values, 7–11, 59, 83, 108, 110, 125–27

best practices, 110, 113

Bloom's Taxonomy, 68

Common Core State Standards. *See* standards

content: as a "heap," 25–27, 85–86; changes in, 135; definition of, *14*, 25; in a multi-class unit, 117, 126; learning, 42, 45, 57;

linked to skills and assessments, 26, 72, 78–79, 81–82; sequencing in a unit, 91, 93

course design: as a system, 85–86; assessments within. *See* assessments, mix of; essential questions for. *See* essential questions, for courses; self-assessing. *See* self-assessment; sequencing, 91, 93–95; within academic programs, 101–8

critical friends groups, 152, 155

cross-disciplinary curriculum, 115–27; benefits of, 115; challenges in creating, 125–27; criteria for effectiveness, 116–17; essential questions and, 117–21; finding topics for, 115; types of, 121–24

curriculum mapping, 47, 97, *98*, 102–5, 112–13, 136–37

drover, 26–27

English/language arts, 17–18, 38, 65–66, 70–71, *76*, 78–79, 86, *87*, 91, *92*, 93, 95, 97, *98*, *103–4*, 105, 108, *109*, 116, *119*, 120, 121, 124, 125–26, 129–34

essential questions: course-level, 87–88; cross-disciplinary, 117–20, 123; examples of, *30*, 31, 38, *39*, 41, *48*, *50*, 70, 74, 78–82, *87*, 94, 117, *118*, 120, 126, 129–33; functions of, 28–29, 86–87, 94, 117; lesson-sized versions

DATE DUE
